Harmful Traditional

Gerry Campbell • Karl A. Roberts
Neelam Sarkaria

Harmful Traditional Practices

Prevention, Protection, and Policing

Gerry Campbell
London, UK

Neelam Sarkaria
London, UK

Karl A. Roberts
University of Western Sydney
Sydney, Australia

ISBN 978-1-137-53311-1   ISBN 978-1-137-53312-8   (eBook)
https://doi.org/10.1057/978-1-137-53312-8

This Palgrave Macmillan imprint is published by the registered company Springer Nature Limited.
The registered company address is: The Campus, 4 Crinan Street, London, N1 9XW, United Kingdom

Gerry Campbell: In memory of my twin sister Karen Marie Campbell who was taken from us aged 16 years. A life tragically cut short and denied the opportunity to enjoy, experience life to the full and fulfil her dreams. Also, in memory of my mum, Catherine Campbell 1929–2011; a loving, hardworking and formidable mother, grandmother and great-grandmother who sacrificed, supported and gave up so much, for so many. Much loved and ever present.

Karl A. Roberts: To my wonderful children, Henry and Matilda, and my fantastic wife, Vicki, each of you makes my life a loving and fantastic journey. And in loving memory of my mum, Jean Roberts 1939–2018, a life well lived. We will always remember and look for you in rainbows.

Neelam Sarkaria: This book is dedicated to my wonderful family and amazing, inspirational mother Bimla Wanti Kapoor who has continued to encourage me to achieve my dreams.

Preface

This book is about harmful traditional practices. Its aim is to provide the reader with knowledge to recognise these abuses and effective ways to respond and prevent them. The authors collectively have a wealth of experience in the fight against these practices sharing expertise in policing, law and psychology. The authors have collected together a detailed account of these practices, their effects and preventative strategies. It is their hope that through the pages of this book, readers will develop their knowledge and be able to confidently respond to the challenges that harmful traditional practices present.

London, UK   Gerry Campbell
Sydney, Australia   Karl A. Roberts
London, UK   Neelam Sarkaria

Acknowledgements

We would like to thank all of our colleagues, teachers, researchers, writers and professionals, past and present working in the field of harmful traditional practice for their support, knowledge and inspiration over the years. Without all of you, this book would not be possible. We wish to acknowledge our families and friends for their constant support and for giving us the time and space to carry out this work. Also, thanks to Palgrave and the team of editors for their understanding and for helping to get this book through to completion. We wish to especially acknowledge all of the survivor and community groups working to end these practices in particular those individuals who, despite threats and their own suffering, show immense courage and leadership and speak out against these practices. Finally, to all victims and survivors of harmful traditional practices, past and present, we hope that your suffering was not in vain and that real change will come soon so that no one else needs to suffer as you have.

Contents

List of Tables

1

Introduction

This book is about *harmful traditional practices*, how they can be identified, challenged and prevented. Within these pages we seek to provide professionals and others with up-to-date knowledge that is useful to their practice and allows them to provide the best possible service to victims and survivors. At the outset it is important to make clear that no matter what the justification presented by supporters and apologists—references to *tradition*, *religion* or *culture*—harmful traditional practices are, as the name implies, all forms of abuse that remove choice, freedom and agency from victims/survivors, cause significant harm to victims/survivors, and are fundamental breaches of a victim's human rights.

The widespread abuse of women and girls (and some men and boys) through systematic disadvantage, violence and other forms of inhuman and degrading treatment, including harmful traditional practices, is a matter of national and global concern. Abuse causes significant personal, financial and social costs impacting upon victims, survivors, witnesses, families, communities and services.[1] These costs include serious physical and psychological injuries to victims and survivors, damage to families and communities, social exclusion and disadvantage and substantial economic loses. This pervades communities, transcending boarders, nationality, culture, gender, sexualities and socio-economic status.

The rates of violence and abuse against women and girls are staggering. In the UK in 2018/19 there are on average 100 domestic abuse murders of women, 12 honour killings, 1.4 million incidents of domestic abuse of which

---

[1] Her Majesty's Government Violence against Women and Girls Strategy 2016–2020.

© The Author(s) 2020
G. Campbell et al., *Harmful Traditional Practices*,
https://doi.org/10.1057/978-1-137-53312-8_1

approximately 750,000 were criminal offences and 450,000 sexual abuse victims/survivors.[2,3,4] In addition, the Crime Survey for England and Wales to year ending March 2019, shows 2.4 million people aged 16–74 years surveyed stated that they had experienced domestic abuse in the previous 12 months. In the same period the police forces in England and Wales recorded 162,030 of which 58,657 were rapes.[5] Research also reveals the high economic cost of domestic violence, including the lost economic output of women, estimated in the UK alone as £66 billion annually.[6] In addition, the cost to health, housing, social service care, criminal and civil justice provision amounts to £3.9 billion per year.[7]

Harmful Traditional Practices

The focus of this book is upon harmful traditional practices, but what are they? To begin, it is important to define some key concepts that will underpin our subsequent discussions. These include providing definitions of *culture*, *cultural practices*, *tradition*, and how traditional cultural practices are differentiated from those that are harmful—so-called *harmful traditional practices*.

There are many definitions of *Culture* and much debate as to which is most appropriate. For the purposes of this book we define culture in accordance with definitions drawn from the field of cross-cultural psychology. Here culture is seen as a set of interrelated values, tools and practices that are shared among groups of individuals who have a common identity. Culture is very important and strongly influences many psychological and social processes, from how an individual perceives, interprets and interacts with situations through to how an individual sees themselves, in particular their sense of who they are and their self-esteem.[8]

[2] Office of National Statistics https://www.ons.gov.uk/peoplepopulationandcommunity/crimeandjustice/articles/domesticabuseprevalenceandtrendsenglandandwales/yearendingmarch2019.

[3] Macfarlane, A, Dorkenoo, E., *Prevalence of Female Genital Mutilation in England and Wales: National and local estimates.* (City University London and Equality Now, 2015).

[4] Balliol, H, *Tackling Female Genital Mutilation in Scotland, A Scottish Model of intervention*, (Scottish Refugee Council and London School of Hygiene & Tropical Medicine, 2014).

[5] Office of National Statistics https://www.ons.gov.uk/peoplepopulationandcommunity/crimeandjustice/articles/domesticabuseprevalenceandtrendsenglandandwales/yearendingmarch2019.

[6] Walby, *The Cost of Domestic Violence Up-date 2009* (Lancaster University, 2009).

[7] Home Office, The economic and social cost of domestic abuse, Research Report 107, January 2019 accessed via https://assets.publishing.service.gov.uk/government/uploads/system/uploads/attachment_data/file/772180/horr107.pdf.

[8] Fiske, A. P., Kitayama, S., Markus, H. R. & Nisbett, R. E. (1998). The cultural matrix of social psychology. In D. T. Gilbert, S. T. Fiske & G. Lindzey (Eds.), *The Handbook of Social Psychology* (4th ed., Vol. 2, pp. 915–981). Boston: McGraw-Hill.

Every culture generates its own series of cultural practices and values. *Cultural practices* have been formally defined as,

> *shared perceptions of how people routinely behave in a culture*[9] i.e. what people should do.

While cultural values have been defined as,

> *shared ideals of a culture*[10] i.e. what people should think.

It is important to note at this juncture that cultures comprise multiple interacting practices and values that can change over time and interact with gender and other characteristics of individuals. In attempting to understand harmful cultural practices it is therefore important not to consider cultures as static or monolithic or to consider the practices as the province of 'other,' 'backward' groups who need to be reformed by a 'wise' West.[11]

Cultural practices and values are important as they are part of the broad behavioural governance of a culture, defining what behaviour is and is not acceptable for its members. Cultural practices and values have a powerful influence upon individuals. Individuals may suffer significant distress, such as loss of self-esteem, anxiety and even shame, if they don't behave in the pre-scribed manner. Indeed, continued membership of a group or the culture itself is often contingent upon behaving in ways that are consistent with the demands of these practices and values. Social exclusion, isolation and damaged self-esteem is a real outcome for those who fail to conform.[12]

It is perhaps true to say that many cultural practices developed because they were broadly adaptive for members of that culture, that is to say were broadly beneficial to all (or some) members of the group. Indeed, certain practices and values may have at one time allowed groups to thrive. For example, strictly mandating practices such as monogamous marriage would be likely to increase the chances of survival of babies born within the marriage. The marriage prac-tice is a socially constructed reason for the mother and father to stay together and increases the likelihood that they will. This in turn means that there

---

[9] Frese, M., 2015. Cultural practices, norms, and values. *Journal of Cross-Cultural Psychology*, 46(10), pp. 1327–1330.

[10] Ibid.

[11] Gill, A. K. (2014) 'Honour' and honour-based violence in Gill, A. K., Strange, C. and Roberts, K., 2014. *'Honour' Killing and Violence*. United Kingdom: Palgrave Macmillan.

[12] See Chap. 2 in, Roberts, K. A., Campbell, G. and Lloyd, G., 2013. *Honor-Based Violence: Policing and Prevention*. CRC Press.

would be two individuals to care for any babies born to that marriage. Two individuals, a father and mother, could work together increasing the likelihood that appropriate food could be found, and other care needs achieved. In the absence of strictly enforced monogamous marriage, there may be no social or other pressure for fathers, especially, to stay with the mother to care for the child, thus raising the risk of a child having to be cared for by a lone parent. To parent alone is significantly more challenging, meaning that some care needs may not be met. This therefore raises the risk of a baby failing to thrive and perhaps of infant mortality.

Other cultural practices were ways to cement group identity by making membership intentionally difficult to achieve. Example of this might include various (physical) trials and rites of passage that marked the point when boys became men, and where group membership was contingent upon successfully navigating these trials. Here, a sense of personal esteem comes from having achieved group membership. This in turn meant that an individual was more likely to have a personal stake in the group's success and this increased the likelihood that they would work in the interests of the valued group.

Where cultural practices and values have been developed, held and repeated by members of a culture over long periods of time (sometimes centuries or more), they often attain the status of *traditions,* that is, traditional practices and traditional values. Thus, members of a culture may talk of concepts such as, 'traditional social values,' 'traditional gender roles' and 'traditional marriages,' and be strongly opposed to any 'new' ideas that could undermine these. Opposition towards new ideas often represents a real fear that the culture and way of life is under threat from the new ideas.

Although some traditional cultural practices were (and are) adaptive for some groups, others disadvantage, and even damage some group members. This may be because, in the modern world, these practices no longer confer the advantages they once did. However, this is often because some practices are (and may always have been) to the detriment of some members of the group relative to others.

Where traditional practices provide no tangible benefit (personal, medical, social or financial) and instead cause harm to the victim, these practices are *Harmful Traditional Practices.* This label highlights the harm the practices cause and the fact that they are motivated and justified by appeals to long-standing values and traditions.

Despite appeals to tradition, cultural or religious needs by those who advocate for or seek to excuse them, harmful traditional practices are fundamentally abuses of the human rights of victims/survivors designed to control their behaviour. All harmful traditional practices are forms of abuse that cause significant harm to women and girls in particular (although some men and boys may also be victimised). The harms can range from physical injury, life-long physical and mental health problems, to death either by suicide, 'forced' suicide or murder. As those most commonly affected by harmful traditional practices are women and girls, it has been argued that one reason for the continuation of many of these practices is that they serve as a mechanism for the maintenance of male authority.[13]

Harmful traditional practices cover a wide spectrum of behaviour and include honour-based abuse (HBA), forced marriage (FM), child and early forced marriage (CEFM), female genital mutilation (FGM), breast ironing, witchcraft, faith and belief abuse, and other related harmful practices.

The Scale of the Problem

Harmful traditional practices are internationally significant problems. The United Nations estimates that annually between 5000 and 20,000 honour killings take place across the world. Although it is important to recognise that the true prevalence of honour killings may never be known as cases may be classed as missing persons or suicide. More than 30% of women in the world today were married before the age of 18 years, and one in nine girls under 15 years of age experience forced marriage.[14] In 2018, the UK Government's Forced Marriage Unit (FMU) gave advice or support relating to a possible forced marriage to 1764 individuals.[15] According to UN estimates, up to 3.8 million girls worldwide are affected by breast ironing.[16] Breast ironing is particularly widespread in the West African nations of Cameroon, Guinea-Bissau, Chad, Togo and Benin. In Cameroon, up to 50% of girls as young as ten years old undergo painful breast ironing on a daily basis. Across the UK it is thought that about 1000 girls within the West African diaspora have been subjected to the practice. The figures could be much higher as there are currently no reliable prevalence data for breast ironing in the UK. The World Health Organisation (WHO)[17] estimated that more than 200 million women

---

[13] Ibid., para 73, p. 29.

[14] International Women's Health Coalition accessed on 6 May 2017 via https://iwhc.org/resources/facts-child-marriage/.

[15] Home Office, Forced Marriage Unit Statistics 2018, May 2019 accessed via https://assets.publishing.service.gov.uk/government/uploads/system/uploads/attachment_data/file/869764/Forced_Marriage_Unit_Statistics.pdf.

[16] http://www.theweek.co.uk/71429/what-is-breast-ironing-and-how-common-is-it-in-britain accessed on13 September 2016.

[17] http://www.who.int/reproductivehealth/topics/fgm/prevalence/en/ accessed on 13 September 2016.

and girls alive today have undergone FGM. Furthermore, there are an estimated 3 million girls at risk of undergoing FGM every year. FGM has been
documented in 30 countries, mainly in Africa, as well as in the Middle East
and Asia, and all Western industrialised nations. Finally, in London, 60 crimes
linked to witchcraft and faith-based abuse were recorded by the Metropolitan
Police Service with many of the cases involving children.

Awareness of Harmful Traditional Practices

Given the scale of the problem, it appears that many professionals are limited
in their awareness and knowledge of harmful traditional practices. In its most
recent report, the UK's Home Affairs Select Committee (HASC), reempha-
sised the importance of professionals in tackling harmful traditional practices
such as FGM.[18,19] However, the HASC also condemned the professions for
submitting incomplete data returns to them and for not complying with the
law in relation to the mandatory reporting of 'known cases' of, just one harmful traditional practice, FGM in girls under 18 years old.[20,21] HASC recommended that tougher sanctions be brought against professionals who fail to
comply with the statutory personal requirement to report and that the duty to
report must not be seen as optional as

> *a decision not to report puts children's lives at risk and is complicit in a crime being
> committed.*[22]

Relatedly, there has been a fall in the number of cases of honour-based
abuse (HBA) recorded by police. In 2018/19 the UK Crown Prosecution
Service reported that the volume of referrals from the police of HBA-related

---

[18] The Home Affairs Committee is one of the House of Commons' departmental select committees. It has
11 Members of Parliament (MPs), drawn from the three largest political parties. The House of Commons
appoints the Committee with the task of examining the expenditure, administration and policy of the
Home Office and its associated public bodies. At the end of an inquiry the Committee will often produce
a 'Government must respond within two months'.

  http://www.parliament.uk/business/committees/committees-a-z/commons-select/home-affairs-
committee/role/.

[19] Home Affairs Select Committee Ninth Report for Session 2016/17: Female genital mutilation: abuse
un-checked.

[20] Regulated Professionals are defined by Serious Crime Act 2015, Section 74(11).

[21] This is a statutory requirement defined by Serious Crime Act 2015, Section 74.

[22] Home Affairs Select Committee Ninth Report for Session 2016/17: Female genital mutilation: abuse
un-checked. Recommendation 12, Para 5.

offences fell to 80 cases from 145 in 2017/18 leading to 72 prosecutions and 41 defendants convicted.[23] One reasons for the drop in recorded offences, given no otherwise change in worldwide prevalence of HBA, could be related to a lack of knowledge on the part of investigators leading to misidentification of cases. Certainly, the number of police investigations referred to the CPS has been falling year-on-year in recent times.[24]

The lack of awareness and knowledge of harmful traditional practices has also shown itself with regard to the sparsity of prosecutions for related offences. For example, the UK has had legislation in place criminalising FGM since 1985, yet there has to date been only been one, ultimately unsuccessful, prosecution for this offence.[25] In its most recent report, the HASC makes a damning assessment of this situation stating:

> It is beyond belief that there still has not been a successful prosecution for an FGM offence since it was made illegal over 30 years ago. This is a lamentable record and the failure to identify cases, to prosecute and to achieve convictions can only have negative consequences for those who are brave enough to come forward to highlight this crime. In the absence of successful prosecutions, FGM remains a national scandal that is continuing to result in the preventable mutilation of thousands of girls.[26]

Given this, there appears to be an urgent need for professionals to be supported with knowledge and information to empower them to recognise harmful traditional practices and the associated warning signs, and for them to act appropriately, especially the need for them to comply with their wider safeguarding duties.

Responses and Prevention

Notwithstanding the scale of the problem, Harmful traditional practices are preventable. However, we need to recognise that no one group can do this alone. Instead, successful prevention requires partnership working. Importantly, this includes strong coalitions of partners drawn from the whole

---

[23] CPS Violence against Women and Girls crime report 2018–2019 accessed on 21 April 2020 via https://www.cps.gov.uk/sites/default/files/documents/publications/cps-vawg-report-2019.pdf.

[24] Ibid.

[25] With the enactment of the Prohibition of Female Circumcision Act 1985.

[26] Home Affairs Select Committee Report for Session 2016/17: Female genital mutilation: abuse unchecked, para 56.

of society where each brings to bear their perspective and contextual expertise. In this book, we will stress the importance of partnership working and the development of coalitions of professionals, including civil society and affected communities,[27] in preventing and tackling harmful traditional practices.

The Present Book

Within this book, drawing on our own experiences, those of other professionals and the wider literature, we aim to provide readers with the knowledge to recognise the perpetration of harmful traditional practices and advice regarding how best to respond. If recognised early, the observable warning signs of harmful traditional practices provide opportunities for effective intervention and prevention; for some individuals this may mean saving their life or preventing repeated harm.

As noted, within these pages we will focus particularly upon HBA, FM, CEFM, FGM, breast ironing, and witchcraft, spirit possession and faith-based abuse. For each of these practices, we describe its characteristics and warning signs, explore its prevalence, its impact upon victims/survivors, relevant legislation and other preventative measures. We also include a chapter describing other less well known and less studied types of harmful traditional practice. The legislation we discuss explores various relevant international treaties and agreements, and national laws, with a particular focus on UK legislation. This is because UK legislation is perhaps more well-developed with respect to some of these practices than in some jurisdictions and is more familiar to the authors. That said, lessons from the UK experience are very much applicable elsewhere. In other chapters we explore approaches to effective police investigation and prosecution of related offences. In our final chapter, we will examine the relationship between harmful traditional practices and alternative dispute resolution mechanisms, the religious courts, Shari'a and Beth Din. Here we identify the characteristics of these alternative dispute resolution systems and various challenges that they present.

Certain types of harmful traditional practice are perhaps more familiar to the reader; these include FGM, FM and HBA. In contrast, whilst there is a

---

[27] Our reference to *affected communities* relates to cultures that are known to perform harmful traditional practices such as FGM, FM, breast ironing and so on. We use this term in contrast to some writers who use the term *practising communities*. This is because, not everyone in affected communities undertakes, supports or otherwise condones the harmful practices, and some members actively campaign against them.

growing awareness of breast ironing as a harmful practice, knowledge of it remains sketchy meaning that it may not be identified. This book is one of the first to explore this form of abuse. Similarly, abuse linked to witchcraft and faith is on the increase and little is currently known about this among many professionals.[28] The abuse generally presents itself as forms of exorcism and witchcraft, victimising both adults and children, and resulting in significant physical and psychological harm, even death. However, half of UK police forces do not record such cases and many local authorities are unable to provide figures about perpetration.

Throughout this book, we have included the accounts of survivors to highlight the impact of harmful traditional practices. These are very important in providing context to this book, and as illustrations of the immense bravery of and suffering endured by survivors. We hope that their accounts of the fear and hurt they have experienced will enable readers to better understand the impact of offending and to galvanise and empower support for them.

One common theme across harmful traditional practices is the lifelong physical and psychological harm to victims and survivors. It is important therefore to acknowledge and respect the immense courage displayed by victims/survivors who come forward to report their experiences. This must never be underestimated. For many, if not all, the decision to come forward is life changing with significant dangers of further abuse from family and community members for their reporting. Because of this, those working to protect victims/survivors often have just one-chance to make the best response, believing victims/survivors and acting appropriately to protect them.[29]

In order to help prevent harmful traditional practices, the associated offending, and to safeguard individuals at risk, we aim to empower readers to recognise the impact, identify the warning signs, and make the most appropriate responses to these practices. The book is designed so that each chapter can be read as a stand-alone account giving the reader detailed familiarity with each of the practices and approaches to them. However, we do hope that readers will explore all of the chapters as each has links with the others and together, they provide as complete a picture as we can provide of the current state of knowledge. It is our sincere hope that empowerment of readers begins within the pages of this book.

---

[28] http://www.bbc.co.uk/news/uk-34475424 accessed on 13 September 2016.
[29] Foreign & Commonwealth Office, Home Office, Multi-agency practice guidelines: handling cases of forced marriage, (June 2009).

2

Honour-Based Abuse and Violence

In this chapter we will discuss honour-based abuse (HBA). Under the umbrella of HBA a range of offending can take place driven by honour-based attitudes and beliefs. We will describe what honour is, how it is applied in unequal and discriminatory ways to males and females, and how honour motivates abuse. This chapter will serve also to provide a context for the other harmful traditional practices discussed in this book.

Terminology

There has been much debate into the appropriate use of terminology to describe abuse related to honour concerns, attitudes and beliefs. There have been consistent objections to the use of the word '*honour*' ('*Izzat*' within South Asian communities), arguing that this term undermines victims and survivors and may give succour to perpetrators by implying that there may be some honour within violence and abuse. Many have argued that there is no honour in abusing others. Some commentators and civil society organisations, such as the UK's Freedom Charity,[1] have called this offending *dishonour violence/crime, shameful violence/crime or shame-based violence*. Other definitions describe it as a form of gender-based violence or a form of violence

---

[1] The Freedom Charity, which was founded in 2009 by Aneeta Prem supports victims of forced marriage, female genital mutilation and dishonour crime.

© The Author(s) 2020
G. Campbell et al., *Harmful Traditional Practices*,
https://doi.org/10.1057/978-1-137-53312-8_2

against women.[2] Such has been the strength of this debate that on 31st January 2017, a UK Member of Parliament, Ms Nusrat Ghani, introduced a private Members' Bill to the House of Commons that sought to prohibit the use of the term 'honour killing' in official publications.[3,4] The Bill was subsequently withdrawn.

Whilst acknowledging this debate, agreeing that there is no honour at all in abusing others, and that the term 'honour' in this context is something of a misnomer, we argue that, in the interests of consistency and continuity, it should continue to be used. This is because 'honour' is now so well entrenched that it is widely understood by communities, policy makers and academics. Especially important here is that consistent use of terminology means that victims and survivors and potential victims and survivors are more likely to understand what is involved and what to do if they have concerns or are under threat of honour-based abuse. We also argue that HBA is not only violence against women and that to refer to it in this way excludes the full range of victimisation. As we shall see, it involves various forms of abuse directed towards females, males and children.

It is also important to note that within this chapter and throughout this book we have used the term *honour-based abuse* (HBA) as opposed to the more common term, *honour-based violence* (HBV). We have done this because we feel that HBA is the best overarching description for the range of crimes (violence and abuses) perpetrated in the name of honour. As well as overtly violent acts towards a victim such as beatings, sexual violence and even homicide, an examination of the range of behaviour carried out in the name of honour includes acts that may be less overtly violent but which are abusive and lead to traumatic consequences to many of their victims and survivors (see the various chapters within this book). This includes acts such as imprisonment, kidnapping, forced marriage, female genital mutilation, breast ironing, exorcism, financial abuse and coercive control to list a few.

We also distinguish HBA from domestic violence and abuse (DV/A). This is because, whilst there are some similarities with DV/A—HBA, like DV/A involves intra-familial offending[5]—the important difference relates to the

---

[2] Hossain, S & Welchman, L, *'Honour': Crimes, Paradigms and Violence Against Women*, (Zed Books, 2005).

[3] Ms Nusrat Ghani is the Conservative MP for Wealden constituency and entered the House of Commons following the general election in May 2015. She is a member of the Home Affairs Select Committee. For further information visit: https://www.parliament.uk/biographies/commons/nusrat-ghani/4460.

[4] Crime (Aggravated Murder of and Violence Against Women) Bill 2016–2017.

[5] The cross-government definition of domestic violence and abuse is: any incident or pattern of incidents of controlling, coercive, threatening behaviour, violence or abuse between those aged 16 or over who are, or have been, intimate partners or family members regardless of gender or sexuality. The abuse can

involvement of the perpetrator's extended family and/or other community members in HBA.[6] Also, in many cases of HBA there may be tacit community support for and concomitantly few attempts at preventing the abuse, especially where other community members share a common concern about honour.[7]

The UK National Police Chiefs' Council (NPCC) helpfully defines HBA as:

An incident or crime involving violence, threats of violence, intimidation, coercion or abuse (including psychological, physical, sexual, financial or emotional abuse), which has or may have been committed to protect or defend the honour of an individual, family and or community for alleged or perceived breaches of the family and / or community's code of behaviour.[8]

We argue that this definition of HBA provides the best operational definition for public authorities, civil society groups and other organisations to work to. This definition more accurately describes the depth and breadth of crimes and abuses perpetrated against victims and survivors in the name of honour.

What Is Honour?

In order to define HBA, it is important to understand what is meant by *honour*. Honour is associated with concepts such as respect and the esteem of others, and self-esteem. Honour can be defined as a positive character trait associated with integrity and good moral character, leading individuals with such qualities to be described as honourable.[9] Being described in this way has advantages, including earning the trust and respect of your peers and may be associated with achieving status and reputation.

Pitt-Rivers[10] highlights that honour has both public and private aspects. Its private aspect relates to an individual's sense of self-worth, and this is strongly

encompass, but is not limited to: psychological, physical, sexual, financial emotional accessed on 21 April 2017 via https://www.gov.uk/guidance/domestic-violence-and-abuse.
[6] Hester et al., Victim/survivor voices – a participatory research project Report for Her Majesty's Inspectorate of Constabulary Honour-based violence inspection (University of Bristol, 2015).
[7] Hossain, S & Welchman, L, *'Honour': Crimes, Paradigms and Violence Against Women*, (Zed Books, 2005).
[8] Ibid.
[9] Vandello, J. A. & Cohen, D, 'Male honor and female fidelity: Implicit cultural scripts that perpetuate domestic violence', [2003] *Journal of Personality and Social Psychology* 84, at p. 997.
[10] Ibid.

influenced by its public aspect. The public aspect of honour is related to the good opinion of others, that is, reputation, how trustworthy an individual is and their perceived status.[11] Honour is very important in honour cultures (those cultures that value honour, see below), precisely because it is intrinsically linked to an individual's reputation and status within a community.

Honour Exists in Many Cultures

In any discussion of honour and HBA, it is important to note that as far as their members are concerned, different groups and communities differ in viewing the relative importance of honour. Some communities can be considered to be honour cultures[12] where the maintenance of personal and family honour is a central organising principle defining the sorts of behaviour that are acceptable and unacceptable. For other cultures honour is less important, although honour concerns and expectations may still have an influence on behaviour. For example, some individuals may be expected to attend particular schools or universities, take up specific occupations to follow family tradition or may marry only within their birth faith, and conforming to these expectations is strongly tied to a sense of familial honour, integrity and wellbeing.

Given that honour concerns can be found in many communities and groups, what is important for our discussion is not that a particular community or group has or even prioritises honour concerns, that is, a so-called Honour Culture, but to examine *how* breaches of honour codes are dealt with. Only where breaches of honour codes are dealt with by abuse or violence can HBA be said to occur. This is very important because it leads to the conclusion that HBA is possible within any culture, nation, community or group that values honour and where individuals respond to challenges or losses of honour with abuse or violence. It is also important to stress given the above point that it is non-sensical, as some commentators have suggested, to locate HBA only within certain nations or cultures, for example, Arab, Kurdish or Pakistan, and to blame any instance of HBA upon members of these communities—so-called othering of cultures.[13] Indeed, a 4-year study of nearly

---

[11] Julian Pitt-Rivers, "Honor and Social Status," in *Honour and Shame: The Values of Mediterranean Society* (eds. J. G. Peristiany, Weidenfeld and Nicolson, 1965).

[12] Ibid.

[13] Bredal, A. Ordinary verse other violence. In Gill, A.K., Strange, C. and Roberts, K., 2014. *Honour Killing and Violence*. United Kingdom: Palgrave Macmillan.

2000 honour killings in Pakistan found that whilst the majority of victims and survivors were from Muslim backgrounds, many were also from Christian and Hindu backgrounds.[14] Similarly, honour is of high significance in many Southern States within the USA where there is good evidence for a Southern Culture of Honour.[15,16] The danger in 'othering' cultures or groups is that HBA is attributed exclusively to unchanging beliefs, customs and characteristics of the 'othered' groups without consideration of individual characteristics or more patriarchal values that underpin much violence especially against women.[17,18]

Gender Roles and Honour

Honour cultures are more likely to value traditional gender roles in which there is discrimination and inequality between males and females.[19] Indeed, codes of honour, whilst being applicable to both males and females, typically place different obligations upon them. Males within honour cultures have political and social power and are expected to protect and defend the honour of others.[20] They are encouraged to develop sensitivity to insults and threats to reputation and are expected to act quickly when their honour and that of their family is being challenged.[21] A failure to do so is seen as weakness and may lead to attacks to destabilise the individual male, their family or group. Male sensitivity to dishonour in honour cultures, especially concerning the behaviour of female relatives, leads them to operate a number of different strategies to control, monitor and limit the behaviour (especially the sexual behaviour) of female relatives. For example, they may limit the ability of females to socialise outside their family or community, to take up paid employment, the

---

[14] Muazzam Nasrullah, Sobia Haqqi, Kristin J. Cummings, 'The epidemiological patterns of honour killing of women in Pakistan' [2009]. *European Journal of Public Health* 19 (2) at p. 193.

[15] Bertram Wyatt-Brown, *Southern Honor: Ethics and Behaviour in the Old South* (Oxford University Press, 1982).

[16] Cohen, D. and Nisbett, R. E., 1994. Self-protection and the culture of honor: Explaining southern violence. *Personality and Social Psychology Bulletin*, 20 (5), pp. 551–567.

[17] Gill, A. K, All they think about is honour. In Gill, A.K., Strange, C. and Roberts, K., 2014. Honour killing and violence. United Kingdom: Palgrave Macmillan.

[18] Nisbett, Richard E., and Dov Cohen. "Violence and honor in the Southern United States." *Guns in America: A Reader* (1999): 264–274.

[19] Heise, L, 'Integrated, Ecological Framework', [1998] *Violence Against Women* Vol. 4, Issue 3, at p. 262.

[20] Ibid.

[21] Fisher et al., 'Field test of the cognitive interview: enhancing the recollection of the actual victims and witnesses of crime' [1986] *Journal of Applied Psychology* 74 (5), at p. 722.

type of work undertaken, their use of public transport, and more broadly their ability to freely make autonomous decisions.[22] Within honour cultures, females are seen as the principal responsibility of the male head of the family and any breach of honour reflects both on the individual and the family head. The head of the family's ability to protect and control the conduct of family members, particularly females, is seen as a representation of his ability to protect his own honour.[23]

Females are expected to maintain their own honour and that of their family through their deference, fidelity, chastity, modesty and purity. Any behaviours perceived not to conform to this are challenged, frequently with acts of abuse.[24] The abuse can be physical, sexual, emotional and psychological (including threats, harassment and intimidation). In addition, breaches of honour codes that go unchallenged are likely to be perceived to be a sign of weakness on the part of males with responsibility for the female.

Honour Abuse and Violence

Honour is maintained by behaving in ways that are consistent with various culturally defined norms and is lost by failing to behave in a manner that is consistent with them (Pitt-Rivers 1966; Bowman 2007). If one behaves in accordance with honour norms, then one maintains a good reputation and one's social status is maintained. This also applies to ones' family. Honour may however be challenged or even lost as a result of behaving in ways that are contrary to honour-based norms.

For those who value honour, loss of honour can be very damaging. There is evidence that loss of honour is keenly felt, accompanied by feelings of damaged reputation, reduced self-esteem and even shame ('*Sharam*' in Southern Asian cultures). Loss of honour may also result in social isolation as others ostracise an individual or their family due to the perceived dishonourable behaviour. See for example Roberts,[25] for a review of the effects of losses of honour.

---

[22] United Nations. 2006. "United Nations In-Depth Study on All Forms of Violence against Women." *Report of the Secretary-General, A/61/122/Add.1*, para. 78.

[23] Roberts, K. A, Campbell, G, & Lloyd G, *Honour-Based Violence, Policing and Prevention* (CRC Press 2014).

[24] Meetoo, V and Mirza, H, 'There is nothing honourable about honour killings: gender, violence and the limits of multiculturalism', [2007] *Women's Studies International Forum*, 30 (3), at p. 187.

[25] Ibid.

To avoid these negative consequences, there is a strong motivation for individuals who value honour to act in ways that minimise the risk of losing it or to attempt to regain lost honour. A variety of acts, some of which are abusive can then result in an individual or family's efforts to maintain or prevent the loss of honour. Breast ironing and FGM, for example, can be thought of as forms of HBA designed to minimise the risk of a family losing honour by reducing the risk of 'problem' behaviours by their daughter. Similarly, forced marriage ensures that a family does not lose honour as a result of a family member marrying an 'unacceptable' person.

Another form of preventing losses of honour can be surveillance. There is evidence of women being 'policed' and 'surveilled' by family, community members or paid or unpaid bounty hunters.[26] Here individuals report back to a family on the movements and behaviour of an individual. For those engaged in surveillance activities, their behaviour also serves them in securing their own status as someone who upholds honourable values. 'Surveillance' can begin at school with a brother(s) or male cousin(s) providing a 'protective' and watchful eye. The control and monitoring of female relatives are such that swift action (usual some form of HBA) will be taken if there are any transgressions from expected behaviour and conduct. From a criminal justice perspective, this monitoring and surveillance behaviour can be classified as stalking and harassment.

Honour-norms may also include an expectation of a violent attack directed towards the perceived source of dishonour.[27] In many honour cultures, men are educated to be sensitive to slights to their honour and there is an expectation that retaliatory action will be swift. Fischer,[28] discussing cultures of honour, noted that:

> from an early age, small boys were taught to think much of their own honor and to be active in its defense. Honor in this society meant a pride of manhood in masculine courage, physical strength, and warrior virtue. Male children were trained to defend their honor without a moment's hesitation—lashing out against their challengers with savage violence.

Often, where honour is perceived to have been lost due to the behaviour of a family member, extreme shame may by experienced by other family

---

[26] https://www.theguardian.com/lifeandstyle/2010/aug/29/taxi-driver-bounty-hunter accessed on 18 April 2017.

[27] Nisbett, R. E., & Cohen, D, *Culture of Honor: The Psychology of Violence in the South (New Directions in Social Psychology)*, (Westview Press, 1996).

[28] Fischer, D. M, *Albion's Seed: Four British Folkways in America* (OU Press, 1989).

members. This may predicate extreme violence. This is because shame consists of strong and often painful feelings about self and this can lead to feelings of extreme anger or rage leading in turn to extreme violence.[29] This can be seen in many honour killings. To illustrate this, we have included two case studies of honour killings where Heshu Yones and Shafilea Ahmed were both killed by their parents (see the case study boxes below).

Victimisation of Males

It is also important to note that although women and girls are significantly more likely to suffer, HBA is also perpetrated against some men and boys. This is often in relation to their 'unacceptable' (to the woman's family) relationship with a female, because of their sexual orientation, their failure to take decisive action to defend the family or community's honour, or where they have failed to carry out the orders of more senior male family members. The abuse can involve physical assault, ostracism, emotional abuse and homicide.

HBA and Religion

HBA is often justified by perpetrators and those who condone it as being a reflection of their cultural traditions or as mandated by their religious beliefs.[31] Some argue that religion allows the moral correction of individuals, and even the use of force against those that do not conform to or are perceived not to conform to religious teachings.[32] However, these claims are simply wrong. No major religion, Christianity, Judaism, Hinduism, Islam or Sikhism supports the use of violence against women and children. Indeed, the Qur'an states that Allah condemns those who change his creation, and that causing any physical harm is unlawful.[33]

---

[29] Tangney, J. P., Miller, R. S., Flicker, L. & Barlow, D. H, 'Are Shame, Guilt, and Embarrassment Distinct Emotions?' [1996] *Journal of Personality and Social Psychology* 70(6), at p. 1256.
[30] Alesha was given a suspended 12 months' imprisonment sentence.
[31] The UN Secretary General's in-depth study of all forms of violence against women, 2006, paras. 66, 69 at pp. 27–28 A/61/122/Add.1.
[32] Qu'ran: 4:119.
[33] Qu'ran: 2:19.

Case Study: Honour Killing of Shafilea Ahmed

Shafilea Ahmed, born in Britain of Pakistani origin, was one of four children born to her father Iftikhar and mother Farzana. Her parents were from a rural Gujrat district village called Uttam. Shafilea was an intelligent, popular and ambitious young woman who wanted to be a barrister. She was murdered at the hands of her parents on the evening of 11 September 2003 at their home in Warrington, Cheshire, UK. Her decomposed body was found the following February over 100 miles away by the river Kent, in Cumbria.

Shafilea was frequently a victim of physical abuse at the hands of her parents, which she had disclosed to a social worker and other professionals. She ran away from home on several occasions to escape the violent abuse she was facing. Her parents' subsequent criminal trial heard that the regular beatings of Shafilea were designed to destroy her developing sense of independence and her desire to lead a 'Western' lifestyle. Her parents deemed that she was bringing shame on the family.

In 2003, Shafilea was drugged and taken on a flight from the UK to Pakistan by her father along with her younger sister and brother. The intention was to force her into a marriage. In order to escape this Shafilea ingested bleach, which resulted in her being hospitalised in Pakistan and then in the UK.

In September 2003, during one of the many beatings at the hands of her father and mother, Shafilea had a plastic bag forced into her mouth suffocating her. Shafilea's mother was heard to say, 'Just finish it here'. Shafilea was never seen alive again. The other children were present in the family home on that night and the actions of the parents were witnessed by another of their daughters.

Shafilea's body was placed into her father's car and driven 100 miles up the M6 motorway to Cumbria where he dumped her body. No one from her family attempted to report Shafilea missing to the police—as often happens in such cases. The other children were told that, if asked, Shafilea had run away, as she had done this previously. One of Shafilea's schoolteachers did however report her missing.

In February 2004, following heavy rain fall, Shafilea's decomposed body was discovered by workmen by the river Kent in Cumbria. She was subsequently formally identified by DNA and clothing.

During the police investigation both parents and other extended family members were arrested. The parents accused the police of discriminatory behaviour and on one occasion stormed uninvited into a police press conference gathered to discuss Shafilea's murder, accusing the police of racism.

Police continued with the investigation and in late 2010 they got a breakthrough following the arrest of Shafilea's sister Rukish aka Alesha who was involved in staging a robbery at the family home.[30] She was an eyewitness to Shafilea's murder and during that arrest disclosed to the police investigators what she had witnessed.

On 7 September 2011, the Ahmeds were charged with their daughter's murder. Following a criminal trial in 2012, they were both convicted of Shafilea's murder and were given a life sentence with a minimum sentence of 25 years each.

During sentencing the judge Justice Roderick Evans said:

(continued)

(continued)

Your concern about being shamed in your community was greater than the love of your child .... However, you could not tolerate the life Shafilea wanted to live.

Before her murder, Shafilea had disclosed details of her abuse to professionals including a schoolteacher, social and homeless worker, to school friends and a male friend. Telling them that she was being physically abused by her parents and had grave concerns about being forced to marry a cousin in Pakistan. A good student, she was however absent from school for days and weeks at a time and regularly had bruising to her face and neck. This leads us to question whether or not effective intervention opportunities were missed in this case.

Prevention

Legislation

HBA is a fundamental abuse of an individual's human rights. This accords with the United Nations' (UN) Convention on the Elimination of All Forms of Discrimination against Women (CEDAW).[34] Despite this, in the UK there is currently no statutory definition or offence of HBA, although as we shall see in later chapters, there is specific legislation regarding female genital mutilation, and forced marriage. Her Majesty's Inspectorate of Constabulary and Fire & Rescue Service (HMICFRS), following its 2015 inspection into so-called honour-based violence, did however recommend that honour-based violence/abuse be made a criminal offence.[35]

Warning Signs of HBA

In attempting to prevent HBA, it is important to understand the victim's cultural background and national origins. This means that to prevent HBA, it is critical for multiagency cooperation and for professionals to engage with communities, NGOs and others. Indeed, the relationship that law enforcement and government officials have with the wider community or distinct sections of it is crucial with respect to assessing such risks.

[34] http://www.un.org/womenwatch/daw/cedaw/cedaw.htm.
[35] Ibid.

There are a number of so-called red flag or trigger events, which may be predicators of honour-related offending taking place. Where these are identified in families or social contexts where honour values are likely to be strong, there is an increased risk of victimisation and professionals need to act swiftly to protect potential victims and survivors . It is important to note that any one of these factors alone are not sufficient to predict HBA, but taken together with due sensitivity to the cultural context, and a focus upon the orientation towards honour of a family and the cultural group to which they are members, can alert professionals to a heightened risk of HBA that should trigger action. We invite the reader to examine the two case studies in this chapter with respect to the warning signs detailed below, as each case features a number of them.

The following are warning signs, consisting of various trigger events and incidents, that can raise the risk of HBA among groups where honour values and beliefs are important, that is, within honour cultures:

- An extra-marital affair.
- An individual seeking a divorce.
- A boyfriend or girlfriend disapproved of by family members.
- Intimacy, sexual relationship and/or pregnancy outside marriage.
- An inter-faith relationship.
- The victim being identified as lesbian, gay, bisexual or transgender.
- Rejection of or escape from a forced marriage.
- Behaviour—notably of females, which is deemed to be inappropriate, for example, inappropriate dress, wearing of cosmetics and similar, kissing or other displays of intimacy, 'being too Westernised';
- A victim reporting her/his abuse to the police and other public authority. In this scenario the risks of abuse to victims and survivors escalate when they report their victimisation.[36]

---

[36] Hester et al., Victim/survivor voices – a participatory research project, Report for Her Majesty's Inspectorate of Constabulary Honour-based violence inspection, (University of Bristol, 2015).

Case Study: Honour Killing of Surjit Athwal

Surjit Athwal was an HM Customs and Excise officer. She was lured to India in 1998 on the pretext of attending family weddings. She was murdered on the orders of her mother-in-law and husband after she sought a divorce.

Following her marriage to Sukhdave, Surjit and her husband lived with his mother and brother. In 1989, Surjit was joined by her sister-in-law Sarbjit after her marriage to Sukhdave's brother. As the matriarch, the mother-in-law ruled the household.

Within her marriage there were many arguments around Surjit's desire to lead a more Western lifestyle. Surjit also suffered repeated domestic abuse. As a result of these experiences, she left the family home. However, she was tracked down by her husband who threatened to kill her if she didn't return home. After returning home, Surjit insisted on socialising with her friends. This angered her husband who physically assaulted her.

Evidence suggests that Surjit's husband had accused her of having an affair and started to follow her to work when she became pregnant with her second child.

At a family gathering her mother-in-law told those present, 'She's [Surjit] bringing shame on the family. We have to get rid of her'. A plan was made to take Surjit to India on the pretext of attending family weddings and a clothes shopping trip.

Sarbjit, Surjit's sister-in-law, aware of the dangers of breaching the family honour code, made two brave efforts to alert the police service. On the day that she was due to travel with her mother-in-law to India, Sarbjit courageously made an anonymous phone call to CrimeStoppers (a UK-based charity) to report that a murder may take place.[37] She followed this up with an anonymous letter to Hayes Police station (Metropolitan Police Service) in London. (Tragically, this letter was found years later, un-opened at the police station).

Two weeks later, Surjit's mother-in-law returned back alone to the UK declaring that Surjit had stayed on in India. A month or so later, she confessed to Sarbjit, that Surjit was put in a jeep with two men on the pretext of going on a clothes shopping. Surjit was drugged, stripped of her jewellery, and her body was discarded into the Ravi River, which runs along the border with Pakistan. Eventually, a report was made to British police by Sarbjit.

The murder investigation was beset by difficulties. For example, false letters were sent to the police in Punjab claiming to be from Scotland Yard, and there were false accounts from witnesses who had allegedly spoken to the victim after the time of her death.

Throughout this time, Sarbjit received direct and indirect threats from the Athwal family. This included a night when her mother-in-law slept in the same bed as her and the following morning stated, 'You've never met our family in India, so I've decided I'm going to take you on a trip'.[38] Following the arrests of

(continued)

---

[37] CrimeStoppers is a UK registered charity, which allows the public to anonymously provide information about criminal activity.

[38] It is apparently common in the Sikh culture to sleep with an older relative. A rejection of such a request is viewed as being disrespectful.

(continued)

her in-laws, Sarbjit reported being assaulted and threatened by her husband to get her to retract her statement.

The expressions of intimidation were not limited to family members. A temple elder approached Sarbjit at a temple and described her mother-in-law as a 'holy woman' and that Sarbjit should tell the police that she was mistaken. This was not an isolated incident as Sarbjit was intimidated and ostracised by other community members.

On 19 September 2007, Surjit's mother-in-law Bachan Athwal aged 70 years and Surjit's husband, Sukhdave Athwal, were convicted of her murder and sentenced to life imprisonment.

The Athwal family, sadly, have been unable to fully grieve as Surjit's body has never been found. Despite her courage, Sarbjit is shunned by community members who believe she has brought dishonour on her family.

Summary and Recommendations

HBA takes many forms, including murder, rape, kidnap, stalking, false imprisonment, coercion, intimidation, threats to kill and many more abuses. We recognise that the UK in particular has been on a long journey regarding HBA and our collective experience and understanding have evolved over time. During this time, there has been much discourse about the use of terminology including the word 'honour' to describe this form of abuse. We argue that the most useful term that describes this form of offending is *honour-based abuse*.

We have noted that all communities have some form of honour code; however, it is when attempts to maintain or defend honour involve harmful practices and result in criminal behaviour and abuses, that the behaviour of individuals involved must be addressed. This means that focus should be on those *individuals* within communities who utilise abuse in order to protect and maintain honour.

As discussed in this chapter, males and females have different roles within honour cultures to protect, defend and maintain individual, family and the community's honour. However, it is evident that women and girls face significant discrimination and inequality by the disproportionate expectations placed on them.

It is of critical importance that all professionals—legal, healthcare, social care, education and law enforcement—and communities are able to recognise HBA and understand their role in safeguarding victims and survivors. In this chapter we have identified a number of warning signs, which could be used to enable early intervention and support for victims and survivors to prevent crime and abuse.

3

Female Genital Mutilation

In this chapter we will discuss female genital mutilation (FGM). We will begin by defining what FGM is and detail its history. We will then explore its worldwide prevalence, its impact, relevant legislation including a discussion of notable FGM prosecutions, and finally, we will explore responses to FGM. At the outset of this chapter, it is important for us to note that, whilst the word 'mutilation,' is used as part of the internationally recognised definition of this practice (and we use it here for clarity), we strongly believe that it is for victims/survivors to define their experience of the act in their own terms.

FGM is a serious form of child abuse and a serious breach of the human rights of victims and survivors, the physical and emotional consequences of which can be devastating and lifelong. It is a global problem, with the number of girls undergoing, exposed to or otherwise living with the consequences of it increasing.[1,2] As a consequence, professionals across a range of disciplines have an important role to play in safeguarding girls at risk. However, many professionals are blind to or ignore the warning signs of FGM. This is illustrated by the fact that, despite FGM being a specific criminal offence since 1985 in the UK, to date there has only been one successful prosecution.[3] There are many reasons for this blindness to FGM. There can be failure to

---

[1] Macfarlane, A., Dorkenoo, E., Prevalence of Female Genital Mutilation in England and Wales: National and local estimates. City University London and Equality Now, 2015.

[2] NHS Digital, Annual statistical publication for FGM during 2018/19 accessed 17 December 2019 via https://digital.nhs.uk/data-and-information/publications/statistical/female-genital-mutilation/april-2018%2D%2D-march-2019.

[3] R v N (Female Genital Mutilation) Sentencing Remarks of Mrs Justice Whipple 8 March 2019.

© The Author(s) 2020
G. Campbell et al., *Harmful Traditional Practices*,
https://doi.org/10.1057/978-1-137-53312-8_3

raise concerns because of a lack of knowledge about FGM, fear of challenging a (barely understood) practice that is considered (incorrectly) to be of religious or cultural importance to its practitioners, or failure to recognise FGM as serious child abuse because it takes place within otherwise loving and non-abusive families, that is, families not normally expected to be at high risk of abusing their children. This chapter therefore aims to raise awareness of FGM, to challenge lack of knowledge and dispel some of the myths surrounding it in the hope that this pernicious form of child abuse may be better identified and prevented.

What Is Female Genital Mutilation (FGM)?

The World Health Organisation (WHO) definition of FGM is accepted as the standard definition. The WHO defines FGM as comprising:

> *all procedures that involve partial or total removal of the external female genitalia, or other injury to the female genital organs for non-medical reasons.*[4]

This definition captures the essence of FGM, stressing the non-medical and therefore abusive reasons for the removal of otherwise healthy tissue. This is the definition of FGM that we will use in this chapter.

Classification of FGM Types

Various different types of genital mutilation occur. In defining FGM, Zwang provides us with a useful description of the anatomical structure of female external genital organs and reminds us of the seriously abusive nature of FGM stressing that any removal of healthy tissue for non-medical reasons is mutilation. Zwang also encapsulates the misogyny inherent in this abuse by highlighting how FGM involves destroying genetically determined and essential anatomical characteristics that are shared by all women and girls.

Zwang stated that[5]:

---

[4] UN, Female genital mutilation, A joint statement by WHO, UNICEF and UNFPA, 1997 accessed on 31 July 2017 via http://apps.who.int/iris/bitstream/10665/41903/1/9241561866.pdf.

[5] 'Mutilations sexuelles feminines. Techniques et Resultants, Female Circumcism, Excision and Infibulation, ed. Scilla Mclean, Minority Rights Group Report No. 47, December 1980.

Any definitive and irremediable removal of a healthy organ is a mutilation. The female external genital organ normally is constituted by the vulva, which comprises the labia majora, the labia minora or nymphae, and the clitoris covered by the prepuce, in front of the vestibule to the urinary meatus and the vaginal orifice. Their constitution in female humans is genetically programmed and is identically reproduced in all the embryos and in all races.

In order to better describe the various types of FGM, the WHO, UNICEF and United Nations Population Fund (UNFPA) produced a typology of FGM. This typology identified four types of FGM.[6] It has since undergone various modifications, incorporating for example a number of typology subdivisions to more accurately describe FGM practices (see Appendix for a detailed breakdown of the typology).

To summarise this typology, the types of FGM are[7] as follows:

Type I—Clitoridectomy: partial or total removal of the clitoris and in rare cases, only the prepuce.

Type II—Excision: partial or total removal of the clitoris and the labia minora, with or without excision of the labia majora.

Type III—Infibulation: narrowing of the vaginal opening through the creation of a covering seal. The seal is formed by cutting and repositioning the inner and sometimes outer labia, with or without the removal of the clitoris.[8]

Type IV—Other: all other harmful procedures to the female genitalia for non-medical purposes, for example, pricking, piercing, incising, scraping and cauterising the genital area.[9]

The severity of FGM and the associated health risk to the victim are closely related to the anatomical extent of the cutting, including both the type and amount of tissue that is cut. The extent of genital tissue cutting generally increases from Type I to III, although there can be exceptions.

---

[6] UN, Female genital mutilation, A joint statement by WHO, UNICEF and UNFPA, 1997 accessed on 31 July 2017 via http://apps.who.int/iris/bitstream/10665/41903/1/9241561866.pdf.

[7] Ibid.

[8] The late Efua Dorkenoo: 'Two sides of the vulva are then pinned together by silk or catgut sutures, or thorns, thus obliterating the vaginal introitus except for a small opening, preserved by the insertion of a tiny piece of wood for the passage of menstrual blood. The girl's legs are then bound together from hip to ankle and she is kept immobile for 40 days to permit the formation of scar tissue. In some cases, no stitching is undertaken.'

[9] UN, World Health Organisation (WHO) Factsheet, 2017 accessed on 31 July 2017 via http://www.who.int/mediacentre/factsheets/fs241/en/.

Type IV comprises a large variety of practices that does not remove tissue from the genitals. Though limited research has been carried out on most of these types, they appear to be associated with less risk of harm than the types I, II and III.

History of FGM

An exploration of the historical context of FGM dispels an often-quoted myth that it is exclusively an African practice. The practice of FGM predates Christianity and Islam. It is believed that genital mutilation was first introduced when the Nile Valley was invaded by militant pastoral nomads, around 3100 BC.[10] In ancient Rome Female slaves had one or more rings put through their labia majora to prevent them having intercourse.[11] In Russia the 'skoptozy' (the circumcisers) conducted female circumcision. The related practice of infibulation has its origins in Ancient Egypt, and an early Christian sect practiced infibulation to ensure perpetual virginity.[12]

More recently, Sigmund Freud performed clitoridectomies as a treatment for neuroses on females in North America and in Europe. He erroneously stated that a

vaginal orgasm was a mark of maturity and the clitoral orgasm must be abandoned[13]

and

elimination of clitoral sexuality is a necessary precondition for the development of femininity.[14]

Nineteenth Century medical texts also proclaimed genital mutilation as an accepted treatment of conditions such as 'nymphomania, hysteria, masturbation, deviance and other non-conforming behaviour'. In London, Dr Isaac

---

[10] Dorkenoo, E., *Cutting the Rose. Female Genital Mutilation: the Practice and its Prevention*, Minority Rights Group 1994.

[11] Ibid.

[12] Female circumcision in Egypt—Current Research and Social Implications, Marie Assad, American University of Cairo 1979.

[13] Morgan. R., and Steinem, G., International Crime of Genital Mutilation first published in *Ms Magazine*, March 1979.

[14] Donohoe, Martin. "Female Genital Cutting: Epidemiology, Consequences, and Female Empowerment as a Means of Cultural Change." *Medscape Ob/Gyn & Women's Health*. 6 November 2006. 11(2). http://www.medscape.com/viewarticle/546497.

Baker Brown justified cutting off the clitoris of some of his patients as a cure for insomnia, sterility and unhappy marriage. In the USA until 1925, a medical association called the Orificial Surgery Society provided training in clitoridectomy and infibulation 'because of the vast amount of sickness and suffering which could be saved for the "quieter sex"'.[15]

Prevalence of FGM

The WHO has estimated that more than 125 million girls alive today in 28 countries in Africa and the Middle East have undergone FGM or some form of genital cutting.[16] The prevalence of FGM appears to be increasing, as more recently UNICEF estimated that at least 200 million girls and women alive today have undergone FGM in 30 countries.[17] FGM is a worldwide phenomenon having been identified in all continents, although it appears to be concentrated in certain areas such as West Africa and among the associated diaspora from these areas. Countries with the highest prevalence of FGM are Somalia 98%, Guinea 97% and Djibouti 93% of the population of women and girls aged 15–49 years.[18]

As noted, FGM also affects women and girls in Western nations. Whilst there is a dearth of data on prevalence in the UK, one study by City University, London, gives an estimate using data drawn from the 2011 UK census for England and Wales. They estimated that about 103,000 women aged 15–49 years, and around 24,000 women aged 50 years and over, who had migrated to England and Wales from 28 countries 'practising' FGM, are living with the consequences of FGM. Further, that around 60,000 girls aged 0–14 years were born in England and Wales to mothers who had undergone FGM and may therefore be at risk of it.[19] It is also important that in this study there were no local authority areas in England and Wales unaffected by FGM.

In the UK, NHS Digital also publishes annual FGM data.[20] This dataset arises because, since 2015 in the UK, it has been mandatory for all clinicians

---

[15] Duffy, J., A Nineteenth Century Answer to Masturbation. The Female Genital/Cutting Education and Networking Project, 1989.

[16] WHO's Factsheet N241 FGM published 2014.

[17] UNICEF, 'Female Genital Mutilation/Cutting: A Global Concern', 2016.

[18] Ibid.

[19] Macfarlane, A., Dorkenoo, E., Prevalence of Female Genital Mutilation in England and Wales: National and local estimates. City University London and Equality Now, 2015.

[20] NHS Digital is the national information and technology provider for the health and care system. It is the new trading name for the Health and Social Care Information Centre (HSCIC). Further information can be found by visiting www.digital.nhs.uk accessed 14 October 2019.

across all NHS healthcare settings to record when a patient with FGM is identified, and what type it is. The key findings from the most recent data published indicates that in the period October 2017 to December 2017, there were 1760 women and girls who had an attendance where FGM was identified or a procedure related to FGM was undertaken.[21] Of these, 1030 were newly recorded women and girls where *newly recorded* means it was the first time they have appeared in this dataset. This data does not however indicate how recently the FGM was undertaken.

Victim Age

The age at which mutilations are carried out varies from region to region.[22] It may be done at a few days old among the Ethiopian Jewish Falashas, and the nomads of Sudan; at around age seven in Egypt and many countries in Central Africa; in adolescence among the Ibo in Nigeria; shortly before marriage or prior to the first child being born as among the Aboh in mid-western Nigeria; or amongst widows as in the Darasa people of Ethiopia. Adult women may also choose to undergo FGM when they are marrying into a different ethnic group, for example, African women from non-practising communities in Southern Sudan who marry northern Sudanese men.[23]

FGM has also been used as a political tool to control women; for example, the UN reported that the so-called Islamic State of Iraq and Syria (ISIS) ordered all girls and women between the ages of 11 and 46 in and around Iraq's northern city of Mosul to undergo FGM.[24] There is however conflicting reports of the accuracy of this report.

Broadly, FGM appears to disproportionately affect young girls. It is troubling to note that in most of the countries highlighted by UNICEF, the majority of girls were cut before reaching their fifth birthday.[25] According to UNICEF's data, 44 million of those who have been cut are girls aged 14 or younger, with the highest prevalence of FGM amongst this age being in

---

[21] The Female Genital Mutilation (FGM) Enhanced Dataset (SCCI 2026) supports the Department of Health's FGM Prevention Programme.

[22] Ibid.

[23] Ibid.

[24] https://english.alarabiya.net/en/perspective/2015/06/04/Study-claims-practice-of-female-genital-mutilation-in-Iran.html accessed on 26 July 2014.

[25] Ibid.

Gambia (56%) and Mauritania (54%).[26] In addition, it is also reported that in Indonesia, around half of girls aged 11 and younger have undergone FGM.

Recent Declines in Prevalence

Thanks in part to various local and regional campaigns by the UN, WHO and other NGOs, there is some evidence that FGM may be declining. In 2016 UNICEF noted that momentum was growing worldwide to address the practice, and that prevalence rates globally among girls aged 15–19 had declined.[27] Since 2008, more than 15,000 communities and sub-districts in 20 countries have publicly declared that they are abandoning FGM, including more than 2000 communities in 2016 alone. Five countries have recently passed national legislation criminalising the practice—Kenya, Uganda, Guinea-Bissau and recently Nigeria and Gambia. The biggest decrease was in Liberia, which saw a 41% decrease for girls in that age group over the last 30 years. Other countries with big declines included Burkina Faso (down 31%), Kenya (30%) and Egypt (27%).[28] Data also appears to indicate widespread disapproval of the practice, as the majority of people in countries where FGM data exists think it should end.[29] Interesting this includes nearly two-thirds of boys and men who are often key decision makers, leaders and influences in patriarchal societies. The United Nations is working to end the practice by 2030 as part of its global development agenda.

However, all that said unfortunately the overall rate of progress in reducing FGM is not enough to keep up with population growth, which will see the number of girls potentially facing FGM increasing as a result of an increasing birth rate. According to UNICEF, if the current trend of increasing numbers of girls being born continues, the number of girls subjected to FGM will increase over the next 15 years.[30]

---

[26] UNICEF, 'Female Genital Mutilation/Cutting: A Global Concern' 2016.
[27] Ibid.
[28] Ibid.
[29] Ibid.
[30] Ibid.

Methods of FGM

There are a range of different methods used in FGM. It is sometimes performed with special knives (among some tribes in Mali, a saw-toothed knife),[31] with a special razor blade known as Moss el Shurfa amongst some tribes in Sudan, or with pieces of glass or scissors. On rare occasions sharp stones are used in Eastern Sudan and pieces of glass or scissors in other areas. Such implements will usually be used for FGM Types I, II and III.

Cauterisation or burning is practiced in some parts of Ethiopia, and fingernails have been used to pluck the clitoris off babies in the Sono areas of the Gambia.[32] These methods of FGM makes it difficult to detect in later life presenting challenges for law enforcement investigators and legal professionals who seek to prosecute offenders.

Perpetrators

Perpetrators moat often include individuals who have culturally defined roles to engage in the practice. Most frequently a traditional birth attendant performs the genital mutilation, for example, the *Daya* in Egypt and the Sudan, while in Somalia FGM 'excisors' are from the Midgan clan. In Nigeria and Egypt male barbers are also known to be involved, although generally a woman who is not the girl's mother traditionally carries it out. In Mali, Senegal and the Gambia woman of the Blacksmith's caste called the Ngansing perform the FGM.[33]

Medicalization of FGM

FGM is known to be practiced in hospitals and other medical establishments in Egypt, Guinea, Kenya, Nigeria, Northern Sudan, Mali, Yemen and Indonesia.[34] The UN reported that in Egypt 82% of FGM cases are

---

[31] Dorkenoo, E., *Cutting the Rose. Female Genital Mutilation: the Practice and its Prevention*, Minority Rights Group 1994.

[32] Serour, G. I., *African Journal of Urology* Vol. 19, Issue 3, September 2013, pp. 145–149.

[33] Dorkenoo, E., *Cutting the Rose. Female Genital Mutilation: the Practice and its Prevention*, Minority Rights Group 1994.

[34] Serour, G. I., *African Journal of Urology* Vol. 19, Issue 3, September 2013, pp. 145–149 accessed on 13 August 2013 via http://ac.els-cdn.com/S1110570413000271/1-s2.0-S1110570413000271-main.pdf?_tid=01cbe8f0-7ffa-11e7-9844-00000aab0f02&acdnat=1502609920_c265805dd6864237d52762490a55b345.

performed by trained medical professionals despite FGM being outlawed there since 2008.[35] Indeed, in these countries there is an upward trend for this.[36,37]

Some trained medical professionals also carry out FGM in settings other than medical establishments. Medical practitioners engaged in FGM have frequently rationalised their behaviour in terms that it reduces the harm and medical risks faced by the girl.[38] However, as a so-called harm reduction and safer approach FGM is not without significant risks. For example, on 29 May 2016, 17-year-old Egyptian Mayar Mohamed Mousa died in a hospital in the Suez region of the country after undergoing 'medicalized' FGM.[39] Rather aptly Vivian Fouad, the head of the Egyptian health ministry programme to combat FGM, called Mayar's death a 'crime committed by criminals known as doctors'.[40] Similarly, in 2013, Sohair al-Bata'a, a 13-year-old died under the care of Dr Raslan Fadl. In January 2015 Dr Fadl, who was the first doctor to be convicted of for an FGM crime in Egypt, was sentenced to two years of imprisonment (although he was subsequently released after three months following his reconciliation with the victim's family—who themselves were complicit in her undergoing the FGM).[41]

Medicalization of FGM isn't confined to Egypt or the African continent. In April 2017, two medical doctors were arrested in Michigan in the USA (Dr Jumana Nagarwala, Dr. Fakhruddin Attar and Dr Attar's wife) for offences relating to the performance of FGM on two 7-year-old girls of Dawoodi

---

[35] UN Egypt, Statement on the death of Mayar Mohamed Mousa, May 2016 accessed on 13 August 2017 via http://www.eg.undp.org/content/egypt/en/home/presscenter/articles/2016/may/un-egypt-statement-on-death-of-mayar-mohamed-mousa%2D%2Dvictim-of-fe.html.

[36] Ibid.

[37] UNICEF, Innocenti Research Centre, Changing a Harmful Social Convention: Female Genital Mutilation/Cutting, p. 7, May 2008 accessed on 13 August 2017 via http://www.unicef-irc.org/cgi-bin/unicef/Lunga.sql?ProductID=396.

[38] Serour, G. I., African Journal of Urology Vol. 19, Issue 3, September 2013, pp. 145–149.

[39] https://www.theguardian.com/world/2017/jan/18/egyptian-judge-gives-four-people-suspended-sentences-over-fgm-death accessed on 13 August 2017.

[40] http://www.independent.co.uk/news/world/middle-east/teenager-dies-during-illegal-female-circumcision-procedure-in-egypt-a709756.html accessed on 13 August 2017.

[41] https://www.theguardian.com/world/2016/aug/02/egyptian-doctor-convicted-of-fgm-death-serves-three-months-in-jail accessed on 13 August 2017.

Bohra[42] background.[43,44] All three are, at the time of writing, currently await-
ing trial. In Australia, a retired midwife and two others, the victim's mother
and a spiritual leader, were imprisoned after two sisters of Dawoodi Bohra
background had undergone FGM sometime between 2009 and 2012. All
three defendants in this case were sentenced to 15 months' imprisonment.[45]

It is noteworthy that both international and national professional bodies
representing medical practitioners have condemned the practice of FGM. For
example, the International Federation of Gynecology and Obstetrics (FIGO),
an international Federation embracing 124 member societies of obstetricians
and gynecologists in the developed and developing world, strongly condemns
all forms of FGM performed by medical personnel or traditional healers in all
countries and all communities around the globe. Noting that they are harmful, unethical, with no medical benefits whatsoever, and are against the code
of medical practice. FIGO also strongly condemns all past, present or future
calls to medicalise any form of FGM/C.

Motivation for FGM

There are many explanations (and myths) for the existence and continuation
of FGM. Various reasons that have been put forward including that FGM is
an important religious practice, that it helps to safeguard purity and virginity
before marriage and chastity after marriage, is important in the prevention of
rape, that it provides a source of income for circumcisers, and it exists for
aesthetic reasons. However as we shall see below, as a form of gender-based
violence the primary motivation driving the perpetration of FGM is that it is
part of the history and cultural tradition of affected communities, where failure to engage in the practice leads to social exclusion and importantly, a loss
of personal and familial honour.[46]

---

[42] In the Dawoodi Bohra community the type of FGM procedure the victims underwent is known as 'khatna', which involves nicking of a girl's clitoris in the presence of female elders.

[43] US Department of Justice Press release on 13 April 2017, accessed on 13 August 2017 via https://www.justice.gov/opa/pr/detroit-emergency-room-doctor-arrested-and-charged-performing-female-genital-mutilation.

[44] US Department of Justice Press release on 21 April 2017, accessed on 13 August 2017 via https://www.justice.gov/opa/pr/detroit-doctor-and-wife-arrested-and-charged-conspiring-perform-female-genital-mutilation.

[45] http://www.abc.net.au/news/2016-03-18/pair-given-jail-time-over-genital-mutilation-of-young-sisters/7257222 accessed on 13 August 2017.

[46] UN Secretary General's in-depth study of all forms of violence against women, 2006, para 1, p. 9. A/61/122/Add.1, para 78, p. 30.

Some communities believe that FGM is a religious obligation, ordained and required by their religion. For example, within Islam, *Suuna*[47] is used to describe a religious tradition or obligation, and this term has been used by some members of the Muslim faith to describe and to justify the act of FGM.[48,49] However, FGM is not mandated or supported by any of the world's major religions with none of them providing any scriptural or other endorsement or justification for it. For example, verse 4:119 of the Qur'an condemns the act of disfiguring or mutilating God's creation as abominable in the sight of God, (indeed this is often cited as evidence for the prohibition of FGM in Islam).[50]

Rather than being a religious practice, FGM therefore appears to be a *cultural* practice related to the particular cultural heritage and needs of its adherents. FGM is seen within some communities as a rite of passage and a practice that *must* be performed. That FGM promotes cleanliness in girls, a 'circumcised' woman is often regarded as spiritually 'pure', disciplined and able to withstand all the hardships that are part of being a woman in her particular society. Performance of FGM on one's daughter is then an important part of the cultural identity of the community—their shared sense of who they are—providing community membership for the girl and all of the associated benefits. It is important to note that notions of *cleanliness* and *purity* associated with FGM have no medical justification.

There are significant costs to both daughters and their families should a family not engage in FGM. For example, a girl who has not undergone FGM may face stigma, discrimination and accusations about perceived promiscuity, bringing shame and dishonour (see the chapter on honour-based abuse in this book) both to herself and her family. She (and her family) may be excluded from community events and activities and the daughter may ultimately be unable to marry because she is 'unclean' and doesn't 'share' an important characteristic of female members of the community.

The cultural basis of FGM has significant implications for the prevention of FGM, and the protection of victims and survivors. Victims and survivors

---

[47] The Arabic word Sunna means 'road' or 'practice' and 'denotes the whole of licit [lawful] practices followed in the Religion (*din*), particularly the pristine (*hanif*) path of Prophets, whether pertaining to belief, religious and social practice, or ethics generally speaking'.

[48] Momoh, C., *Trends in Urology and Men's Health* Vol. 15, Issue 3, May/June 2010, pp. 11–14.

[49] National FGM Centre, Traditional Terms for female genital mutilation, accessed on 13 August 2017 via http://nationalfgmcentre.org.uk/wp-content/uploads/2017/06/FGM-Terminology.pdf.

[50] Chishty, M. Former National Police Chiefs Council's Lead for FGM, 'FGM is not Religious but Ritualistic.'

face a difficult choice in whether or not to report their families and communities to police. On the one hand, their victimisation may be prevented if they speak to police (or other professionals). On the other hand, reporting the threat that they face is likely to result in significant costs to them and their family including ostracism or future isolation, and place them at risk of retaliation by family and community members alike. Also, some victims and survivors do not want to criminalise their parents or demonise their cultural and/ or religious groups, this is especially significant given how negatively such crimes are reported in the Western media.

In discussing the motivation for FGM, it is interesting also to explore the barriers against it that can be harnessed in preventative work. For example, during their work with affected communities, the authors have often heard from FGM survivors that they will not allow their girls to undergo FGM and this is for a multitude of reasons including:

- it is a crime,
- is a fundamental abuse of human rights,
- damages a girl's life chances,
- disempowers girls and
- has lifelong physical and psychological impacts.

However, despite their best intentions or wishes, some mothers are not always capable or able to protect their daughters from the practice due to the strength of social pressure from other family members and/or their wider community. There is evidence of cases of FGM where a mother may be unaware that her child has had it practiced upon her. This happens when another female relative, usually an aunt or grandmother, has 'control' of the child during some time period, for example, a school holiday, and believes that the child has reached an age that she should be 'cut'. The risk here is greater if the child is separated from her mother and resides with these relatives in a country or community where FGM occurs. In an attempt to combat this risk, a new offence was established within the Serious Crime Act 2015 of *Failing to Protect a girl from risk of FGM*.[51]

The importance of culture as a motivation for FGM and the suffering it causes is clearly illustrated in the words of Hawa Daboh Sesay describing her experiences in the case study below.

---

[51] Serious Crime Act 2015, Section 72 accessed on 31 July 2015 via http://www.legislation.gov.uk/ukpga/2015/9/section/72#section-76-3.

Case Study: Hawa Daboh Sesay,[52] Founder and Executive Director of Hawa Trust Ltd.

I became a victim of FGM at 13 years old in Sierra Leone. My memory is that of my old auntie who came and took me to the Northern Province. In the morning they took me to the stream, where I saw lots of women dancing and singing. Before I knew it, I was thrown on the floor. I then felt a sharp pain and started bleeding. That memory cannot be erased from my mind.

It was not until when I came to have my own children that I realised it was because of the FGM that childbirth was difficult for me. I also experienced acute health and psychological problems. The procedure is usually carried out in a bush in secret. This has left me in agony. The thought of the operation in which I nearly bled to death at age 13 still traumatises me and it left me with lifelong physical problems and psychological trauma.

I am therefore determined to make sure my daughter does not experience the same trauma I went through. I explained to her the danger of the practice, and that following our traditions does not mean we must follow FGM practices. I have gone with my daughter to Sierra Leone many times, but I ensure she is protected and does not go near the old women. She has realised the suffering I have experienced and joins me in the anti-FGM campaigns.

It is a traditional thing to prepare for womanhood that has been going on for ages. I am calling on countries practising FGM to work for social change. We should not be followers of those traditions that go against human rights—we are the people who decide, and we are the ones who make the traditions. Traditions are not sent from God—we have the right to change cultures and we should change them. I will always condemn FGM and send a challenge to those who use religion as an excuse to mutilate girls.

The trauma and devastating impact it had on me has led me to form the Hawa Trust in order to address issues of FGM related to HIV and AIDS.

FGM and Honour-Based Abuse

As discussed in the previous chapter on honour-based abuse, violence can occur when perpetrators perceive that a relative or community member has *shamed* the family and/or community by breaking their honour code.[53] As FGM is often a deeply ingrained traditional practice, failure to engage in it and/or should a victim report victimisation to police or others, this is very

---

[52] Hawa is a qualified and registered social worker. She works for Tower Hamlets Social Services, as a locum social worker in the family support team.

[53] National Police Chiefs' Council (NPCC) Honour Based Abuse, Forced Marriage and Female Genital Mutilation Strategy: a policing strategy for England, Wales & Northern Ireland – Eradicating Honour based Abuse, Formed Marriage and Female Genital Mutilation Together (2015–2018).

likely to be perceived as bringing dishonour to the victim's family and the community. Honour has then to be regained and this can lead to a violent attack upon the victim.

Effects of FGM

FGM poses a significant risk to the short- and long-term health of victims and survivors . The WHO lists a range of short- to longer-term health consequences (see the case study of Sophia and Table 3.1) associated with the practice of FGM.

Case Study: Sophia 16 Years Old

Sixteen-year-old Sophia was pregnant and had not undergone FGM. Seven months into her pregnancy her mother took her from their Kenyan village and travelled the short distance to Tanzania where FGM is not illegal—so that Sophia could undergo FGM. Having then undergone Type III FGM, Sophia and her mother travelled back to their village, where Sophia and her unborn child went into shock and she suffered significant blood loss. Sophia was rushed to the nearby medical clinic who couldn't safely manage her injuries. She was then rushed to Loitokitok hospital where she later died.

Following Sophia's death, her family rushed to the hospital to collect her body and bury her immediately before news got out. However, news reached two FGM activists in the area, who reported it to the media. The Director of Public Prosecutor's office were alerted as FGM is unlawful in Kenya and arrests were made.

Sophia's father was acquitted after stating that he had been separated from the mother and was not aware of the circumstances. The 'cutter' from Tanzania was never charged as FGM is not a crime in her country and the offence took place outside Kenyan jurisdiction. The mother reported that it was Sophia who wanted to undergo FGM and she was merely travelling with her daughter. The mother asked for the forgiveness of her community, who rallied around her with support and collected money to pay for her small fine.

The health effects of FGM can include death caused by haemorrhage or infections such as tetanus and shock.[54] A WHO-led study of more than 28,000 pregnant women in six African countries found that those who had undergone FGM had a significantly higher risk of childbirth complications, such as caesarean section and postpartum haemorrhage, than those without

---

[54] UN, WHO, Health Risks of female genital mutilation, accessed on 31 July 2017 via http://www.who.int/reproductivehealth/topics/fgm/health_consequences_fgm/en.

Table 3.1   Immediate and long-term health consequences of female genital mutilation

Immediate health risks	Longer-term health risks
• Severe pain	• Need for surgery
• Shock	• Urinary and menstrual problems
• Haemorrhage (i.e. excessive bleeding)	• Painful sexual intercourse and poor quality of sexual life
• Sepsis	• Infertility
• Difficulty in passing urine	• Chronic pain
• Infections	• Infections (e.g. cysts, abscesses and genital ulcers, chronic pelvic infections, urinary tract infections)
• Death	
• Psychological consequences	• Keloids (i.e. excessive scar tissue)
• Unintended labia fusion	• Reproductive tract infections
	• Psychological consequences, such as fear of sexual intercourse, post-traumatic stress disorder, anxiety, depression
	• Increased risk of cervical cancer (although more research is needed)
Known obstetric complications/ risks	**Conditions often considered to be associated with FGM but for which evidence is equivocal or shows no link**
• Caesarean section	
• Postpartum haemorrhage	
• Extended maternal hospital stay	
• Infant resuscitation	• HIV (in the short term)
• Stillbirth or early neonatal death	• Obstetric fistula
	• Incontinence

FGM. In addition, the death rate for babies during and immediately after birth was higher for mothers with FGM than those without. The risks of both birth complications and neonatal death increased relative to the severity of the FGM type.

Sexual problems are also more common among women who have undergone FGM. They are one and a half times more likely to experience pain during sexual intercourse, have significantly less sexual satisfaction and are twice as likely to report a lack of sexual desire.[55] Although it is important to note that some campaigners in the UK have testified that despite the trauma of the FGM procedure, women who have undergone FGM have been able to recover the capacity for sexual pleasure, including orgasm.[56] There have also been

[55] Berg R, Denison E, Fretheim A. Psychological, social and sexual consequences of female genital mutilation/cutting (FGM/C): a systematic review of quantitative studies. Oslo, Nasjonalt Kunnskapssenter for Helsetjenesten, 2010.

[56] Nimko Ali https://inews.co.uk/opinion/comment/nimco-ali-dont-share-fgm-images-child-abuse-527400.

some benefits noted following surgical clitoral restoration and repair for women living with FGM; these are detailed by the WHO.[57]

There are also significant psychological problems associated with FGM. The initial traumatic effects of FGM include fear, helplessness, horror, anxiety, terror, humiliation and feelings of betrayal. Many women who have undergone FGM suffer from ongoing, serious psychological distress, psycho-sexual difficulties and social stigmatisms related to the effects of this ritual surgery. Despite the physical and mental health consequences, many women avoid seeking health support. This is because the effects of FGM are often ignored, dismissed, normalised or attributed to other causes by both family members and some medical practitioners. These effects of FGM are also rarely discussed outside of the family. Certainly, efforts to de-stigmatise seeking health support for the effects of FGM would help dismantle negative attitudes that prevent women from seeking support. A summary of the immediate and longer-term health effects of FGM are given in Table 3.1.

The fear of FGM can take a significant toll on potential victims and survivors and their desire to escape. This can itself lead them into dangerous situations as can be seen in the case study concerning nine-year-old Mary.

Case Study: Mary, Nine Years Old[58]

Mary, a nine-year-old girl, lived in a Kenyan Maasai Manyatta. One night she overheard her parents discussing her imminent FGM ceremony and marriage to a much older man in the village. Terrified, Mary decided to run away from home as she had previously heard about two girls from a neighbouring village who had also run away to safety. Mary ran 22 kms through the Amboseli national park at night, a place inhabited by dangerous predators including hyenas and lions. Mary was aware of the dangers but felt this was a risk worth taking. Mary was eventually spotted by Kenyan Wildlife Service personnel who picked her up. Mary was transferred to the Divinity Foundation's rescue centre for safety, protection and care.

At the time of her rescue Mary had never been to school and spoke only Maa. She is now slowly starting to understand and converse in Swahili and English and is actively participating in singing and poetry reading sessions. She has made great strides in integrating with the other girls living in the rescue centre and is making good progress in her education.

---

[57] Dr Jasmine Abdulcadir for the WHO https://www.who.int/reproductivehealth/topics/fgm/interview/en/.

[58] Mary is a pseudonym, given to the victim to protect her true identity.

Prevention of FGM

Community Solutions

Throughout this book we stress the importance of partnership working through the development of a coalition of professionals, civil society and affected communities, in preventing and tackling harmful traditional practices.[59],[60],[61] As with other harmful practices, the community has a crucial role in identifying and driving the solutions for change.[62]

It is also important to note that within affected communities, particularly those that are highly patriarchal, males have a fundamental role to play in preventing and eradicating honour-based abuse such as FGM. This is because males often have leadership roles in political, economic and various social structures.[63]

Legislation is also an important tool in the prevention of FGM and this is discussed below.

Legislation

As with all of the harmful cultural practices in this book, FGM is a fundamental breach of the human rights of women and girls. These rights are embodied in the Human Rights Act, the European Convention on Human Rights (ECHR) and the EU Charter on Fundamental Rights. These rights are also set out in a number of international treaties such as Convention on the Elimination of all forms of Discrimination Against Women (CEDAW), the International Covenant on Civil and Political Rights (ICCPR), the International Covenant on Economic, Social, and Cultural Rights (ICESCR), the Convention on the Rights of the Child (CRC) and the Convention Against Torture (CAT).

---

[59] It is important to note that not everyone in affected communities is undertaking, supporting or otherwise condoning the harmful practices and many members actively campaign against them.

[60] National Police Chiefs' Council (NPCC), Honour-Based Abuse, Forced Marriage and Female Genital Mutilation: A Policing Strategy for England, Wales & Northern Ireland 2015–2018, (December 2015).

[61] Home Affairs Select Committee Ninth Report for Session 2016/17: Female genital mutilation: abuse un-checked.

[62] HM Government, Ending Violence Against Woman and Girls Strategy 2016–2020, March 2016 accessed on 20 August 2017 via https://www.gov.uk/government/uploads/system/uploads/attachment_data/file/522166/VAWG_Strategy_FINAL_PUBLICATION_MASTER_vRB.PDF.

[63] The UN Secretary General's in-depth study of all forms of violence against women, 2006, Section B The broad context and structural causes of violence against women, p. 28, A/61/122/Add.1.

On 20th December 2012, The UN General Assembly passed a Resolution where it called upon States in the strongest terms to end this practice, no matter if the mutilation was carried out in or out of a hospital.[64] The Resolution also emphasised that custom, tradition or religious beliefs cannot be used as an excuse for avoiding the obligation to eliminate violence against women and girls.[65]

FGM is a specific criminal offence in many jurisdictions around the world. In the UK it has been criminalised since 1985 with the introduction of the Prohibition of Female Circumcision Act 1985 (the 1985 Act).[66] This Act was subsequently repealed in 2004 in England, Wales and Northern Ireland with the enactment of the Female Genital Mutilation Act 2003 (the 2003 Act) and the Female Genital Mutilation (Scotland) Act 2005.[67] These acts gave extra-territorial effect or jurisdiction, to deter people from taking girls from the UK overseas for the purposes of FGM, and increased the maximum penalty for FGM from 5 to 14 years of imprisonment.

There have been further recent amendments to the UK legislation with the introduction of the Serious Crime Act 2015 (the 2015 Act).[68] The key change here was the introduction of *mandatory reporting* to the police service by health, education and social care professionals (defined as regulated professions) of 'known cases' of FGM.[69] In addition, the Children Act 1989 stipulates that local authorities have a general duty to safeguard and promote the welfare of children within their area who are 'in need' and to promote the upbringing of such children by their families by providing a level of services appropriate to those children's needs.[70] Thus professionals across a range of disciplines including the public and private sector, have a fundamental role to play in safeguarding and protecting girls at risk of FGM.

---

[64] UN, General Assembly 67th Session, Intensifying global efforts for the elimination of female genital mutilations, 2012, A/RES/67/146 accessed on 12 August 2017 via http://www.un.org/en/ga/search/view_doc.asp?symbol=A/RES/67/146.

[65] Ibid.

[66] Prohibition of Female Circumcision Act 1985 accessed on 30 July 2017 via http://www.legislation.gov.uk/ukpga/1985/38/contents/enacted.

[67] The Female Genital Mutilation Act 2003 was brought into force on 3 March 2004 and repealed and re-enacted the provisions of the 1985 Act.

[68] Serious Crime Act 2015, Sections 70–75.

[69] Required by Serious Crime Act 2015, Section 74.

[70] Children Act 1989, s17.

Female Genital Mutilation Protection Orders (FGMPO)

Section 5a and Schedule 2 of the 2003 Act makes provision for FGM protection orders (FGMPO).[71] The purpose of an FGMPO is to protect a woman or girl who is at risk of being subjected to an FGM offence, or against whom such an offence has already been committed. An application for an FGMPO is made to the family court or High Court.[72,73] An FGMPO can also be made on the family court's own initiative where other family proceedings are before the court. Similarly, it can be made in criminal proceedings for FGM offences, either where the defendant is acquitted of an offence, but the court deems that there is a risk, or where the defendant has been convicted but continues to pose a risk. This risk may be in relation to the victim of the offence before the court or any other girl, for example, a sister.

In order to address safety concerns for the girl or other persons involved in making the application, the system allows for:

- orders to be made without notice to the respondent where the court considers it just and convenient, for example, where a girl would be at risk of harm or removal from the jurisdiction if notice were given. This is known as ex parte without notice.
- the possibility of giving evidence by video link from another court centre
- the possibility of applying to redact or withhold portions of evidence on a hearing-by-hearing basis where disclosure would place a person at risk.

FGMPOs might include a range of requirements, commonly these might be:

- requirements for an offender or potential offender to surrender their passport or any other travel document[74]
- requirement not to apply for a passport or other travel document without the leave of the court[75]

---

[71] HM Courts & Tribunals Service, Form FGM700, Female Genital Mutilation Protection Orders accessed on 14 August 2017 via https://formfinder.hmctsformfinder.justice.gov.uk/fgm700-eng.pdf.

[72] Home Office Multi-agency statutory guidance on female genital mutilation, April 2016.

[73] The process for applying for an FGMPO can be found here: https://www.gov.uk/female-genital-mutilation-protection-order.

[74] It is essential to seize all travel documents. It is Important to know therefore whether or not the person or persons is/are dual passport holders. Passports relating to foreign countries can also be seized.

[75] If this control or restriction is imposed, it is essential that the UK Passport Authority is informed as the UK Border Force so that their systems can be updated.

- requirement not to enter into any arrangements, in the UK or abroad, for FGM to be performed on the person to be protected
- requirement not to harass, intimidate or threaten a person(s) either directly or indirectly
- requirement not to associate with identified individuals
- requirement not to enter a specific geographic location in the UK or elsewhere
- perhaps controversially, measures can include a requirement that a person who is at high risk of FGM to undergo a medical examination

FGMPOs can last for a specified period or remain in force indefinitely until they are varied or discharged. This can allow for long-term protection where a girl at risk is very young. It is important, in terms of adequate prevention of FGM that the prohibitions, restrictions and requirements of FGMPOs are regularly reviewed.

For FGMPOs to be most effective it is imperative that they are *logged, monitored* and *checked regularly* by the police service to ensure that their requirements are still current. We recommend that every such order is notified to the police service and the police service ensures that the provisions of the order are placed onto the Police National Computer (PNC) and to the Police National (Intelligence) Database (PND) so that the UK's law enforcement agencies have 'sight' of the orders and the provisions and controls in them. Monitoring and review can be undertaken with or without the direct support of the girl or woman being protected using a diverse range of policing options including the use of covert surveillance techniques. It can also be carried out in partnership with other trusted stakeholders.[76] Care should, however, be exercised in sharing information, particularly if there is any risk of it leading to reprisals against the victim, other members of their family, or others providing support.

The breach or suspected breach of the FGMPO can either be reported to the police as a criminal matter, which carries a power of arrest, or dealt with as a civil contempt of court. The breach of a FGMPO carries a 5-year prison sentence and/or a fine on indictment, or 12 months' imprisonment and/or a fine on summary conviction. If a person is convicted, their conduct can also be dealt with as a contempt of court.[77]

---

[76] Home Office, Multi-agency statutory guidance on female genital mutilation, April 2016 https://www.gov.uk/government/publications/multi-agency-statutory-guidance-on-female-genital-mutilation accessed 14 October 2019.

[77] http://www.legislation.gov.uk/ukpga/2015/9/part/5/crossheading/female-genital-mutilation/enacted accessed on 14 October 2019.

Prosecution of FGM

To date in the UK there has only been one prosecution of an FGM-related case. It also demonstrated the interplay between FGM and other harmful cultural practices, in this case witchcraft.[78] The two defendants were jointly accused of subjecting the girl to FGM by 'deliberate cutting with a sharp instrument' at her mother's home in the presence of her father. Medics raised the alarm when the girl was taken to Whipps Cross hospital in North London with severe bleeding and a surgeon concluded the child had been cut with a scalpel. The defendants claimed their daughter had been reaching for a biscuit when she fell and cut herself on the edge of a kitchen cupboard. Medical experts however, confirmed the cause of her injuries were consistent with cutting rather than a fall. The victim later told police that she had been cut by a 'witch'.[79] While the parents were on bail, police searched the mother's home and found evidence of witchcraft, including spells aimed at silencing professionals involved in the case.

It is interesting in this case that those prosecuting and defending relied on the WHO classification of FGM to underpin their interpretation of the FGM legislation (the court was required to consider whether WHO classification of FGM type IV constitutes 'significant harm') highlighting the absence of clear definitions of FGM within the legislation itself.[80]

The dearth of prosecutions for FGM in the UK highlights the difficulties this crime presents for prosecutors. This as noted appears to be related to failure of recognition among professionals and a related unwillingness of victims and survivors and witnesses to come forward. In this context it is likely to be useful to consider the characteristics of successful prosecutions from other jurisdictions to identify potential learning that is transferable to the UK.

---

[78] There have been three other trials in the UK involving FGM—two in London and one in Bristol—all of which ended in acquittals.

[79] https://www.theguardian.com/society/2019/feb/01/fgm-mother-of-three-year-old-first-person-convicted-in-uk accessed 14 October 2019.

[80] R v Dr Dhanuson Dharmasena and Hosan Mohamed. On 4 February 2015, both were found not guilty of FGM Act and related offences regarding a female patient at the Whittington Hospital in North London. Dr Dharmasena, an obstetrics and gynaecology registrar, was alleged to have performed reinfibulation on a woman after she had given birth. Dr Dharmasena said that he had never before treated a woman who had previously undergone FGM, nor had he received any relevant training. He performed a single suture to stop postpartum bleeding.

Spain

The Spanish Criminal Code was amended in 2003 (Article 149) and a new criminal offence introduced, genital mutilation (male and female). This statute was amended in 2005 in order to give Spanish courts extra-territorial jurisdiction to allow them to hear FGM cases (Article 23.4). The first case taken to court was in 2013. It was a case about two girls, one born in The Gambia and the other one in Spain. The girls lived in The Gambia between 2007 and 2009, while their parents stayed in Spain. In 2008, the mother was informed about the initiation of a magistrate's investigation into FGM and told that she must notify the authorities when the girls returned to Spain. In 2010, a gynaecological examination was performed on the girls, but no anomalies were found. Six months later, a change in one of the girls was detected, 'an alteration to the external female genitals that looked mutilated'. It was estimated to have been afflicted at some point during those six months. The Provincial Court in Barcelona eventually ruled that the parents were criminally responsible for clitoridectomy performed on both their daughters. The parents were each sentenced to six years in prison. The written judgement stated:

> 'The couple deliberately mutilated their young daughters either directly or through a person of unknown identity' and 'Female circumcision is not a culture. It is mutilation and discrimination against women'.[81]

Switzerland 2008

On 30 September 2011, the Federal Assembly of the Swiss Confederation modified its penal code to explicitly ban FGM. In 2008, a couple of Somali origin were convicted for FGM (type Ib, removal of the clitoris) of their elder daughter when she was aged two. It was carried out by a Somali physician, paid 250 Swiss francs, who performed the procedure under local anaesthesia on the kitchen table. The cutting was apparently 'desired' by the mother. The father was against the complete removal of his daughter's external genitalia, arguing for a symbolic intervention. Therefore, they both agreed on the removal of the clitoris. During an interview with the media, the father declared

---

[81] Sentencia del Tribunal Supremo (Supreme Court), STS 835/2012 de 31 de Octubre.

that, it felt 'normal' to them to let his daughter be 'cut'. The parents received a two-year suspended prison sentence by the Cantonal Court of Zurich for having encouraged FGM.[82]

Sweden 2006[83]

In 1998 the Swedish FGM legislation was revised with a change in terminology, from 'female circumcision' to 'female genital mutilation', and more severe penalties for breaking the law were imposed. The law was further changed in 1999, to allow for prosecution in a Swedish court of someone performing female genital mutilation in a country where it is not considered criminal.[84] Since 1982, two cases have been taken to court and both ended in custodial sentences.

A 16-year old girl with Somali-born parents told her school welfare officer that she had been physically abused by her mother. The mother had used different objects to beat her daughter and the beating had been going on for several years. The girl said that she feared for her life as her mother had attacked her with a frying pan while she was asleep. The girl also told the welfare officer that, five years earlier during a visit to Somalia, her mother had subjected her to FGM. She also said that her mother had performed several genital examinations on her to ensure that she was still a virgin. The school welfare officer reported the case to the social authorities who reported it to the police. Medical examination showed an injury to the girl's clitoris corresponding to type I in the WHO classification. Her mother was sentenced to three years of imprisonment for FGM and grievous violation of integrity.

Australia[85]

All States and Territories have passed criminal legislation prohibiting female genital mutilation. These laws also apply extra-territorially to protect Australian citizens and residents from being subjected to FGM overseas. As noted previously, in Australia, a retired midwife and two others, the victims and survivors' mother and a spiritual leader, were imprisoned after two sisters

---

[82] Article 24, the Swiss Criminal Code.

[83] Mölndals tingsrätts dom 2006-10-02 i mål B854-06 (Decision of the Mölndal District Penal Court).

[84] This change in the Swedish law has seen the removal of the principle of double incrimination.

[85] R v A2; R v KM; R v Vaziri (No. 23) [2016] NSWSC 282 18 March 2016.

of Dawoodi Bohra background had undergone FGM. All three defendants were sentenced to 15 months' imprisonment.[86] However, on appeal the defendants successfully argued that the 'cutting' was purely symbolic and medical examination revealed no injuries to the children concerned. The appeal was upheld, quashing the convictions. Since the appeal the High Court, in a split decision, held that the court of appeal erred in quashing the conviction because the intention of the law was to criminalise all forms of FGM, including so-called 'symbolic' acts. At the time of writing the case has been referred back to the court of appeal for further consideration.[87]

Egypt[88]

FGM was made unlawful in Egypt in 2008 through federal legislation. As noted above, an Egyptian doctor was convicted on appeal and sentenced to two years in prison for manslaughter and three months in prison for performing the FGM procedure. The victim's father was also given a three-month suspended sentence for procuring FGM.

France[89]

There is no French legislation outlawing FGM, but it is a crime under articles of the Penal Code, which deal with the mutilation and abuse of minors. Mutilation and abuses such as FGM are punishable by 10 years in prison or up to 20 years for cutting a girl under the age of 15. The law also applies to parents who send French-born children abroad to be cut. The first conviction was secured in 1988 against a father and his two wives, who were each given a three-year suspended sentence. In 1991, a 'cutter' was jailed for five years. Two years later, a mother was jailed for the first time and given a three-year sentence, two years of which were suspended.

---

[86] http://www.abc.net.au/news/2016-03-18/pair-given-jail-time-over-genital-mutilation-of-young-sisters/7257222 accessed on 13 August 2017.

[87] http://www.abc.net.au/news/2016-03-18/pair-given-jail-time-over-genital-mutilation-of-young-sisters/7257222 accessed on 13 August 2017.

[88] http://europe.newsweek.com/fgm-egypt-souheir-al-batea-jail-485168?rm=eu accessed on 17 August 2017.

[89] http://news.trust.org//item/?map=france-reduces-genital-cutting-with-prevention-prosecutions-lawyer/ accessed on 17 August 2017.

Switzerland

In the first Swiss case of its kind, a Somali woman from canton Neuchâtel was sentenced to eight months' prison over the genital mutilation of her two daughters.[90] The law in Switzerland as it relates to FGM outlines that: 'Offences committed abroad are also liable to punishment'. The penal provision set down in Article 124 of the Criminal Code is intended to prevent girls from being taken to their home countries, or to some other country, in order for genital cutting to be carried out. It is not necessary for the accused to have legal domicile in Switzerland in order to be subject to criminal prosecution.

FGM and Political Asylum

Many countries including the UK have passed legislation prohibiting FGM, but this does not necessarily mean that State protection will be provided to those at risk of this harmful cultural practice. FGM continues in many nations and, where there is cross community FGM perpetration, authorities are often unable to prevent, prosecute and punish perpetrators. In such situations, internal escape and relocation are not an option for many and so fleeing a country is one of a few safe options.

The UN High Commissioner for Refugees (UNHCR) Guidance Note states that in determining whether there is an internal flight or relocation alternative in cases involving FGM, it is necessary to determine whether such an alternative is both relevant and reasonable.[91] Where the claimant is from a country with a universal (or near universal) practice of FGM, internal flight will normally not be considered a relevant alternative. The lack of state protection in any part of the country is taken as an indication that the state will not be able or willing to protect the girl or woman in any other part of the country.

Despite this, deportations of vulnerable girls at risk of FGM are still regularly taking place from the UK and Europe.[92] There are many reasons for this. Research into women's asylum claims in Europe has shown that decision makers often apply too high a standard of proof of the risk of FGM, often

---

[90] https://www.endfgm.eu/news-en-events/press-releases/response-statement-landmark-fgm-prosecution-case-in-switzerland/ accessed 19 April 2020.

[91] UN High Commissioner for Refugees (UNHCR), *Guidance Note on Refugee Claims relating to Female Genital Mutilation*, May 2009, accessed on 13 August 2017 via http://www.refworld.org/docid/4a0c28492.html.

[92] https://www.theguardian.com/commentisfree/2019/sep/25/britain-girls-fgm-female-genital-mutilation-asylum-immigration accessed 14 October 2019.

requiring independent evidence that is often virtually impossible for victims and survivors to obtain. This has included, requiring evidence from individuals and groups with country-specific expertise, to establish that FGM is commonly practiced in a particular country. In addition, decision makers are also often insensitive to the impact of shame and trauma upon victims and survivors caused by their experiences of FGM.

Female Genital Cosmetic Surgery

In discussing FGM it is also important to consider the issue of female genital cosmetic surgery (FGCS). FGCS includes labiaplasty (surgical removal of the labia minora), hymenoplasty (reconstruction of the hymen) and vaginoplasty. The Royal College of Obstetricians and Gynaecologists (RCOG) has defined FGCS as a procedure, which is by definition, non-medically indicated (i.e. not necessary for physical or mental health).[93]

There is much debate around whether or not Female genital cosmetic surgery (FGCS), where it involves excision, infibulation or other mutilation of the labia majora, labia minora, or clitoris, is an offence and prohibited under the 2003 Act. This is an issue that will continue to challenge policy makers tasked with interpreting the legislation. The essential question here is whether it was the UK Parliament's original intention to interfere with the autonomy of those women over the age of 18 years who choose to have such procedures. A Home Affairs Select Committee (HASC) report in 2014 called the laws governing FGCS ambiguous.[94] In its report HASC stated,

> We cannot tell communities in Sierra Leone and Somalia to stop a practice which is freely permitted in Harley Street.[95]

In December 2014 the then Home Secretary, Theresa May, was reported to have said,

> doctors who carry out 'designer vagina' cosmetic surgery could be committing a criminal offence, unless there is a physical or mental health justification ... and that

---

[93] The Royal College of Obstetricians and Gynaecologists (RCOG), Ethical considerations in relation to female genital cosmetic surgery, October 2013 accessed on 13 August 2017 via https://www.rcog.org.uk/globalassets/documents/guidelines/ethics-issues-and-resources/rcog-fgcs-ethical-opinion-paper.pdf.

[94] Home Affairs Select Committee, Second Report of Session 2014/2015, Female genital mutilation: the case for a national action plan, 2014, accessed on 13 August 2017 via https://publications.parliament.uk/pa/cm201415/cmselect/cmhaff/201/20102.htm.

[95] Ibid.

courts could be asked to rule whether 'purely cosmetic surgery' falls into the same category of crime as female genital mutilation.[96]

The HASC asked the Government to explore whether there is a case for prohibiting all such surgery on girls under the age of 18, except where it is clinically indicated. There are currently no plans for this change to be made as the Government does not accept that any ambiguity exists.

Police forces in England and Wales have investigated cosmetic surgeons on suspicion of committing offences under the 2003 Act and referred numerous cases to the Crown Prosecution Service (CPS) for decisions regarding prosecution. We argue that, as the law currently stands, FGCS is contrary to the 2003 Act and should be tested within the criminal court system and the legislation as written does apply equally to women and girls.

Certainly, this issue needs to be dealt urgently. Members of affected communities argue that legislative ambiguity means that there is inequitable treatment of girls subjected to FGM. In essence a state of affairs where girls from non-affected communities can attend private clinics for FGCS with the support of their parents without safeguarding professionals being alerted. It was the Association of Chief Police Officers and the Metropolitan Police who argued in 2014 at the Home Affairs Select Committee that there is a perceived 'double standard' whereby there is a focus on practising black and ethnic minority communities, whilst in the wider community, the 'designer vagina' private medical industry is flourishing. This view was supported by campaigners such as Nimko Ali who gave evidence at this Committee.

Academic discourse has considered whether female genital cosmetic surgery appeals to a cultural fantasy of 'normality', or what it means to be a 'normal' woman. Camille Nurko has recently argued that this norm is enmeshed in heterosexuality and the two-sex/gender system, which also regulates other forms of cosmetic cutting of the genitals: specifically, surgery on ambiguous intersex infant genitals and ritual female genital cutting (or FGM). It acknowledges that what it means to be 'normal' is culturally and racially inflected and offers a critical examination of the cosmetic procedure of 'clitoral reconstruction' surgery for women who have undergone ritual clitoral excision. In offering reconstructive surgery to African women, white plastic surgeons divert black feminist political action away from self-definition and autonomy and towards dependence on white benevolence.

---

[96] http://www.independent.co.uk/news/uk/politics/designer-vagina-surgery-could-be-as-illegal-as-fgm-theresa-may-warns-9915466.html accessed 20 January 2020.

Summary and Recommendations

FGM is an act of abuse and is a fundamental abuse of a victim's human rights. It causes significant physical and psychological suffering in victims and survivors and serves no useful medical purpose. Despite statements to the contrary by its adherents, there is no religious justification for FGM. It is an act driven by cultural concerns relating to family honour, and erroneous perceptions of the chastity and cleanliness of the victim.

As we have seen, FGM is a worldwide problem and is not confined to certain locations or religious groups. However, despite its widespread criminalisation the practice still continues, often driven by family members keen to avoid losses of family honour and associated personal and social stigma, and ostracism should their daughter fail to undergo it.

Ultimately, successful investigation, prosecution and prevention relies upon strong multi-partner relationships between different professional groups and especially close engagement with communities affected by FGM. Indeed, it is affected communities that have been shown to be crucial as they can provide information about perpetration and are often best placed to identify and develop method to successfully eliminate it.

Perhaps the last words of this chapter should fittingly be given to Alimatu Dimonekene, survivor and campaigner. Her words powerfully sum up the experience of victims/survivors making clear that their voices should not be disregarded in discussions of FGM. She highlights the important work of campaigners and sends a powerful message of hope for the future.

Alimatu Dimonekene, Survivor and Campaigner:

FGM and its reoccurring complications and pain is never far behind in the life of its victim. I am no different. Despite years of support the struggles continue. Each day comes with its own challenges. But knowing I now have the power to change how I feel is the best part. The role of an activist has given me access to so many women and girls like me, who we all share the same thoughts and emotions on the subject of FGM has helped me in some ways combat the psychological impact.

Campaigning for these many years and speaking constantly with practitioners and stakeholders, communities alike in the UK and elsewhere has also helped to reduce the many obstacles FGM affects women like myself find in talking about our experiences.

Though the campaign has its own twists and uncertainty, voices of those that have gone through FGM must not be side-lined or removed from the main discourse. Ending harmful traditional practices such as FGM, Child Marriage the 'experts' are the victims and survivors themselves. The future of the next generation lies in the way FGM is seen today through their voices and contributions to the campaign.

I am still very much convinced that FGM will end in a generation. Because in my engaging in the fight against FGM my daughters will never undergo the pain I was subjected to and for this I am eternally grateful and proud to have worked with great people such as the late Efua Dorkenoo OBE, Dr Comfort Momoh MBE, Joy Clarke, Janet Fyle MBE and many more.

4

Forced Marriage

In this chapter we explore forced marriage (FM). We will examine in detail what a forced marriage is and the implications for the victims and survivors and their communities. We will differentiate FM from arranged marriage and discuss other forms of illegal marriage such as sham marriages. We will examine the legal framework as it relates to forced marriage and will discuss some of the methods of prevention including legislation such as forced marriage protection orders and their application.

It is important to include forced marriage in a discussion of harmful cultural practices because it is a corruption of the culturally driven practice of marriage creating significant harm. Forced marriages are often associated with honour-based abuses as a failure to marry or an attempt to escape from a marriage leads to a powerful sense of dishonour among other family members. Indeed, there is strong evidence that forced marriages are often predicated upon significant psychological and physical abuse of the victims and survivors. Similarly, where individuals refuse a forced marriage or where they attempt to escape from a forced marriage, significant abuse, including fatal violence, is common.

What Is a Forced Marriage?

A forced marriage is a marriage in which one or both spouses do not give informed consent to the marriage. Tactics used to force someone into a marriage can take many forms including physical, psychological, financial, sexual

© The Author(s) 2020
G. Campbell et al., *Harmful Traditional Practices*,
https://doi.org/10.1057/978-1-137-53312-8_4

and emotional pressure.[1] There is evidence for the perpetration of a wide range of serious crimes to force individuals into marriage. For example, offences recorded by the police in the service of forced marriage include murder, solicitation to murder, kidnap, false imprisonment, wounding, affray, assault, battery, sexual assaults, threats to kill, threats to property and harassment. The lack of consent and abuse used to ensure the marriage is contrary to various international protocols concerning human rights and marriage-related legislation. It is also a criminal offence in the UK and other jurisdictions.[2]

What Is Marriage?

In considering forced marriage it is important also to consider what a marriage is and the legal basis for marriage. This will then allow us to consider how legal marriages differ from those that are forced and other forms of illegal marriage such as sham marriages.

Marriage is a formal union and legal contract between two individuals that ties them together legally, economically, emotionally and socially. In some relationships, and especially within cultures that have a strong honour code (see the chapter on honour-based abuse), a marriage also gives legitimacy to sexual relations between a man and a woman.[3]

International Protocols Relevant to Marriage

The international community has developed various agreements that are designed to protect the rights of individuals. These include the Universal Declaration of Human Rights (UNDHR),[4] European Convention on Human

---

[1] HM Government Multi-agency practice guidelines, *Handling cases of Forced Marriage* (June 2014).

[2] The UN Secretary General's in-depth study of all forms of violence against women, 2006. A/61/122/Add.1 (2006), para 20 defines Violence Against Women as 'any act of gender-based violence that is directed at a woman because she is a woman or acts of violence which are suffered disproportionately by women'.

[3] Roberts, K. Campbell, G. & Lloyd, *Honor-Based Violence Policing and Prevention* (CRC Press, 2013), p. 18.

[4] http://www.un.org/en/universal-declaration-human-rights/ accessed on 21 February 2016.

Rights (ECHR).[5] These agreements are all clear that marriage should be between adults who have consented to marry, and that individuals have a right to divorce. Relevant also to marriage are various conventions designed to eliminate discrimination against women and violence against women. For example, The Convention on the Elimination of All Forms of Discrimination against Women (CEDAW) and the Istanbul Convention on preventing and combating violence against women and domestic violence. These are all relevant to forced marriage as they prohibit use of coercive practices to force women to behave in particular ways, and activities that impinge upon the human rights of women. Clearly, forced marriage breach all of these conventions and agreements.

The Law Governing Marriage in the UK

In this section, we consider marriage law in the UK. We do not examine all aspects of the UK's marriage legislation but deal with the sections relevant to forced marriage. There are important differences in legislation between England and Wales, Ireland and Scotland and we will highlight these. We will also illustrate where these differences may be exploited by those engaged in forced marriage. Same-sex marriages and civil partnerships are outside the scope of this book.

For marriages to be valid in the UK as a whole, they must be:

- monogamous
- consensual
- be carried out in accordance with the requirements of the relevant legislation, for example, Marriage Acts 1949 & 1994, Matrimonial Causes Act 1973 (for England & Wales) and Marriage (Scotland) Act 1977

These provisions, by definition, outlaw the concept of forcing individuals to marry.

England and Wales

There are two ways to marry in England and Wales: a religious or belief ceremony, or a civil ceremony. Marriages must take place in an appropriate

---

[5] http://www.echr.coe.int/Documents/Convention_ENG.pdf accessed on 21 February 2016.

location such as a register office, other approved premises, or in a place of religious worship that has been officially registered by the Registrar General for England and Wales. Except for marriages in the Church of England or the Church of Wales, each party to the marriage must give notice in person—at least 28 days before the ceremony—to the Registrar Superintendent (of the district where she/he lives). A marriage must be solemnised within 12 months of giving such notice in a registered or regulated place (as described) and in the presence of a Registrar or an Authorised Person. This includes a priest or Imam who will register the marriage and issue a marriage certificate. Marriages conducted overseas in accordance with the proper formalities required by that country's laws are generally recognised in England and Wales (and elsewhere in the UK), provided both parties have the legal capacity to marry. However, there is no automatic right of recognition.

Religious ceremonies conducted in accordance with the UK's laws mean that there is no need for couples to have a civil marriage.

However, if a religious marriage ceremony takes place in a church, mosque or temple, which is not an authorised place or is conducted by a person who is not authorised to conduct weddings, then a marriage is not legal under the Marriage Act 1949, whether or not notice of the marriage has been given. The law also allows for a religious blessing to be given after a legal civil ceremony. In addition to the above, a party to a marriage must give notice to a designated register office if one of the intended spouses is from outside the European Economic Area or Switzerland.

The minimum age at which a person is able to consent to a marriage is 16 years old; however, a person under the age of 18 is unable to marry without parental consent.[6] It is possible that legal caveat of parental consent could, naively, support the practice of forced marriage. This is because, it is generally the parents who are the prime motivators in forcing their children to marry against their wishes, and they may claim that their otherwise underage children, had their consent. It is therefore essential that the person conducting the marriage ceremony *satisfies* themselves as to the true and informed consent of any 16- to 17-year-olds who are to be married.

A marriage can be annulled where either party did not validly consent to it, through duress, mistake, unsoundness of mind, or otherwise.[7] A petition for a decree of nullity based on lack of consent must be brought within three

---

[6] (Unless that person is a widow/widower) Matrimonial Causes Act 1973 s11(a)(ii).
[7] Matrimonial Causes Act 1973 s12(c).

years of the marriage date.[8] It is important to note therefore that a forced marriage remains valid *until* it is voided in nullity proceedings.

A particular challenge in attempts to prevent forced marriage is the use of technology. According to the UK's Freedom Charity, some Imams in the UK have been conducting wedding ceremonies over the internet using Skype.[9] In one case, an 11-year-old home-educated girl from London was married on Skype to a 25-year-old man in Bangladesh.

Scotland

The Marriage (Scotland) Act 1977 and Marriage and Civil Partnership (Scotland) Act 2014 are the statutes regulating marriage in Scotland. Historically, the law of marriage developed differently to other UK jurisdictions because of the differences in Scottish Law and the role of the established Church of Scotland. There are two ways to marry in Scotland:

1. *A religious or belief ceremony*:
   Such marriages may .take place anywhere and may be solemnised by an 'authorised celebrant', for example, Church of Scotland Minister, other minister of religion, clergyman, pastor, priest, or *other person approved to do so under the Marriage (Scotland) Act 1977, s 8(2)*. Immediately after the solemnisation of the marriage, the Marriage Schedule shall be signed by the parties to the marriage, by two witnesses present to the signing, and by the celebrant. The parties to the marriage must, within three days, deliver the Marriage Schedule to the district registrar who will enter the details into the register of marriages.
2. *A civil ceremony*:
   A civil marriage may take place in a registration office or at *any place* agreed between the registration authority and the couple and may be solemnised by an 'authorised Registrar', that is, a registrar or an assistant registrar who has been authorised by the Registrar General for that purpose. [Section 8 (2) Marriage (Scotland) Act 1977].

A significant difference with other parts of the UK is that *anyone aged 21 years or over* may become an '*authorised celebrant*' or '*temporary authorised*

---

[8] Matrimonial Causes Act 1973 s 13(c).
[9] https://www.easterneye.eu/skype-forced-marriage-growing-trend/ accessed on 23 July 2017.

celebrant' under Sections 9 or 12 of the Marriage (Scotland) Act 1977. In the case of the former, the applicant must also be a member of a religious body. However, the temporary 'authorised celebrant' *does not* need to be a member of a recognised or established religious body.

This poses a potential opportunity for those trying to procure a forced marriage. For example, it would be possible for someone sympathetic to a forced marriage to register as a celebrant to conduct a wedding. It is important therefore that the relevant authorities to exercise due diligence in granting temporary authority and adequately explore the background and motives of anyone wishing to do this.

Another key difference with the rest of the UK is that in Scotland, individuals who are aged 16 or 17 years old *do not have to have parental consent* to get married and any two persons, *regardless of their gender or residence*, may marry in Scotland.[10] Thus any 16- or 17-year-old (subject to the conditions listed below) can go to Scotland to get married *without the consent of their parents*. Other conditions that must be met to marry in Scotland are that the individuals:

- are not related to one another in a way which would prevent their marrying, for example, an incestuous relationship.
- are unmarried and not in a civil partnership.[11]
- are capable of understanding the nature of a marriage ceremony and of consenting to marrying.
- the marriage would be regarded as valid in the party's country of domicile.
- Notice must be given in the three-month period prior to the date of the marriage and not later than 29 days before that date.

As regards forced marriage, this again presents a potential opportunity for those wishing to achieve this as individuals may marry in Scotland without being resident there, and there is an opportunity for those under 18 years old to be married.

---

[10] www.nrscotland.gov.uk accessed on 30 March 2016.

[11] If a person is in a qualifying civil partnership, they can change it to a marriage. A qualifying civil partnership is a civil partnership, which was registered in Scotland, England, Wales or Northern Ireland and has not been dissolved, annulled or ended by death or an overseas relationship registered outside the UK, which is treated as a civil partnership in Scotland and has not been dissolved, annulled or ended by death.

Northern Ireland

Northern Ireland has similar provisions for marriage as those in force in England and Wales. The exception being that there is currently no legislative basis for the provision of same-sex marriage.

Marriage and Shari'a Law

In Shari'a law, marriage is regarded as a legal and social contract between a man and a woman that is witnessed by two other Muslim people. The age at which individuals can get married is whenever the individuals feel ready, financially and emotionally. This therefore raises an area of conflict with UK domestic legislation in that the age of consent for marriage could be disregarded.

Arranged Marriage

When discussing forced marriage, one must draw the clear distinction with an *arranged marriage*. In arranged marriages, the families (parents or older family members) of both spouses, or a third person such as a matchmaker, take a leading role in identifying and introducing the respective parties to the union and will make the marriage arrangements. The prospective bride and groom can get to know each other via email, telephone, social media, and/or through a series of dates (chaperoned and unchaperoned) before they decide if they are right for each other. However, importantly *the choice* of whether or not to accept the proposal remains *solely* with the prospective spouses. Informed consent means that the person consenting to the marriage must be able to understand their decision and choice and has the mental capacity to do so.[12] Arranged marriages have existed for generations. They have taken place within European Royal Families and the aristocracy to resolve wars and other disputes, as business transactions, to build wealth and form alliances.

---

[12] http://www.legislation.gov.uk/ukpga/2005/9/section/3 accessed on 6 March 2016.

Relationship Between Arranged and Forced Marriage

Although, in principle, there is a clear distinction between what is an arranged and a forced marriage, it is true that attempts at arranged marriage may become forced marriages. It is therefore our contention that arranged marriages and forced marriages are linked on a continuum defined by coercion and consent. This view is echoed by An-Na'im,

> it may therefore be useful to see both arranged and forced marriages as arranged but falling on a continuum between consent and coercion. This characterization acknowledges the cultural and contextual nature of consent and considers its difference from coercion as a matter of degree and perception, with persuasion playing a key role in the grey area of the continuum.[13]

As the parents or older family members take a leading role in an arranged marriage, they will seek potential spouses that allow them to realise their family's key aims, in particular enhancing, retaining or increasing status and wealth. It is likely that there are circumstances in which one or other of the prospective spouses may be unwilling to accept the union. The key question then is what a family will do in response to reluctance to marry. At one end of our proposed arranged–forced marriage continuum the wishes of the prospective spouses are accepted, and the union does not go ahead. At the other end, a family uses abusive tactics to ensure compliance and the marriage goes ahead regardless of the wishes of one or other of the prospective spouses, a forced marriage.

The point at which an arranged marriage might be classified as a forced marriage need however to be explored. As noted, where tactics that are themselves criminal offences such as physical force, sexual abuse, kidnapping, false imprisonment and so on are used to obtain compliance, then it would be acceptable to call any resulting marriage a forced marriage even if it started as a lawful arranged marriage.

However, what are other forms of 'persuasion' that may be used to obtain compliance? At what point does a family's, perhaps legitimate, attempts to encourage compliance, mould into abuse? If an individual subsequently consents to an arranged marriage after experiencing 'persuasion' where violence and threats have perhaps not been used, is this free informed consent? Some

---

[13] An-Na'im, A, *Forced Marriage* (SOAS University of London, 2000).

families might argue that they have a legitimate right to attempt to persuade other family members to behave in ways that might be 'good' for them and this may result in a 'change of mind'. If this results in marriage, is this a case of forced marriage? Identifying what is legitimate family behaviour is the point at which arranged marriage moulds into forced marriage on our continuum.

We argue that in order to best assess whether a marriage is forced or whether a family's behaviour has been within acceptable bounds, it is important to place the responses of the victim at the centre of our decision making. This respects the human rights of potential victims and survivors of abuse and allows us to tease out the legitimate from illegitimate activities. Perhaps then, along our continuum from arranged to forced marriage there is a point where 'acceptable' forms of persuasion give way to coercion and this must be judged by the effects that this has on the victim. In this regard the psychological and physical state of the victim becomes important. Repeated persuasion , especially from significant persons such as parents, even if it's non-violent, has psychological effects on an individual that may cause various forms of psychological disorder. Indeed, failing to accept an individual's opinion and repeatedly attempting to undermine it, no matter how 'gently' this is done, can have a significant impact damaging self-esteem and provoking anxiety and depression. This is because the sense of autonomy and self-efficacy of the individual is repeatedly challenged and undermined. How long it takes for someone to develop psychologically significant symptoms varies between individuals, so the duration is less significant than the effects of persuasion attempt upon the victim.

If we look at the impact of their experience upon victims and survivors: were an individual to suffer psychological or psychiatric injury (or indeed physical injuries) as a result of their family's activities, this could delineate the point where legitimate attempts to change someone's mind mould into abuse, that is, if a marriage results the point that delineates a forced marriage. An offence in England & Wales was created by the Anti-Social Behaviour Crime and Policing Act 2014, Section 121 (1) and in Scotland under Section 122 of the same Act, enshrines some of these considerations.[14] This statute permits victims/survivors of the forced marriage crime to 'own the crime' by being able to express the effects their family's behaviour has had upon them.[15] The

---

[14] http://www.legislation.gov.uk/ukpga/2014/12/section/121/enacted accessed on 23 July 2017.

[15] Jasvinder Sanghera is the founder and CEO of Karma Nirvana, a UK-registered Charity that supports victims of Forced Marriage and Honour-Based Abuse. It was established in 1993.

UK Crown Prosecution Service legal guidance[16] on offences against the person describes a serious psychiatric injury as an infliction of grievous bodily harm, contrary to the Offences Against the Persons Act 1861, Section 20, that is a very serious assault. The case study below describes the legal view in the UK of psychiatric injury; although not related to forced marriages, it shows how seemingly non-abusive behaviours may result in these injuries.

Case Study: Psychiatric Injury *R v Ireland [1997] 3 WLR 534*[17]

The defendant made a series of silent telephone calls over three months to three different women. He was convicted under Offences Against the Person Act 1861, Section 47. He appealed, contending that silence cannot amount to an assault and that psychiatric injury is not bodily harm. His conviction was upheld. The court ruled that silence can amount to an assault and psychiatric injury can amount to bodily harm.

Prevalence of Forced Marriage in the UK

There is currently no independent estimate of the prevalence of forced marriage in the UK. The best available data comes from the UK Government's Forced Marriage Unit. Recent figures of the number of forced marriages can be seen in Table 4.1. The estimates suggest that between 1200 and 1800 forced marriages occur annually. These are figures for the number of reported

Table 4.1 Prevalence of forced marriage in the UK

Year	Number of cases	% female/ male	% under 16 years old	Total % under 18 years old	Number of disabled/LGBT victims and survivors	Number of different countries involved
2012[a]	1485	82/18	13	35	114/22	60
2013	1302	82/18	15	40	97/12	74
2014	1267	79/21	11	22	135/8	88
2015	1220	80/20	14	27	141/29	67
2016	1428	80/20	15	26	140/30	90
2017	1196	78/21	15.6	29.7	125/21	65
2018	1764	75/17	17.7	32.6	193/11	74

[a]https://www.gov.uk/government/uploads/system/uploads/attachment_data/file/141823/Stats_2012.pdf accessed on 23 July 2017

[16] http://www.cps.gov.uk/legal/l_to_o/offences_against_the_person/ accessed on 6 March 2016.

[17] http://www.e-lawresources.co.uk/R-v-Ireland.php accessed on 20 August 2017.

cases and may therefore substantially underestimate the true prevalence. For example, many victims/survivors are unable to report their victimisation for various reasons such as the fear of abuse. Also as discussed below, there are credible reasons to suspect that many males do not report their victimisation.

Both women and men are forced into marriages. However, women and girls are predominately the victims/survivors of this harmful traditional practice.[18] The Forced Marriage Unit's (FMU) data highlights that on average 81% of those contacting the Unit are female.

Evidence also suggests that LGBT people may be forced into marriage to conceal, 'cure' or 'correct' their sexual orientation and/or their gender identity from other family members and their communities.[19]

There is also evidence highlighting that people with learning disabilities are forced into marriage. It is suspected that there are a number of reasons for this including[20]:

- parents wishing to find a partner/carer for their disabled adult children;
- a person with learning disabilities may be seen as easier to deceive, coerce into or consent to such a marriage and into then acting as an immigration visa sponsor;
- they may be less likely to protest or challenge the request to marry; and
- families may believe that marriage will allow a person with learning disabilities to lead a 'normal' life.

As noted above males may be less likely than females to report their victimisation. There are a number of reasons why this may be so. Men often don't want to report their experiences of forced marriage because of fear of not being believed, being stigmatised, ridiculed, or fear of being perceived as weak. In addition, some LGBT men (as well as women) may also fear that their sexual orientation or gender identity might be exposed.[21]

The FMU's statistics also highlight that forced marriage is a global problem. There were 74 countries (see Table 4.2) involved in the FMU's cases and this indicates the need for a transnational action plan to tackle and eradicate forced marriage.[22]

---

[18] Ibid.

[19] EU Agency for Fundamental Freedoms, 2014.

[20] http://www.anncrafttrust.org/Forced_Marriage.php.

[21] Home Affairs Committee, *Sixth Report of Session 2007–08, Domestic Violence, Forced Marriage and 'Honour'-Based Violence* (May 2008), Vol. II, Appendix 3, para 15.

[22] HM Government, *Ending Violence against Women and Girls Strategy, 2016–2020* (March 2016).

Table 4.2 Country of origin data for UK forced marriages[a]

Country involved in FMU cases	2014 (1267 cases) %	2015 (1220 cases) %	2016[b] (1428 cases) %	2017 (1196 cases) %	2018 (1764 cases) %
Pakistan	38.3	59	43	36.7	43.6
Bangladesh	7.1	13	8	10.8	8.9
India	7.8	7	6	6.9	6.2
Afghanistan	3.0	–	3	1.6	2.5
Somalia	1.6	–	3	7.6	2.6
Turkey	1.1	–	1	–	–
Iraq	0.7	–	1	1.2	2.0
Iran	1.0	–	1	–	–
Nigeria	–	–	1	1.0	–
Sri Lanka	1.1	–	1	–	–
Egypt	–	–	>1	1.5	0.6
Saudi Arabia	–	–	1	0.9	–
Yemen	–	–	–	–	–
Gambia	–	–	–	–	–
Morocco	–	–	–	–	–
Ukraine	–	–	–	–	–
Tunisia	–	–	–	–	–
Romania		–	–		2.4
Unknown	3.5	–	–	7.0	13.3
Overall number of countries involved	88	67	90	65	

[a]The numbers shown against the relevant countries are percentages of the total number of forced marriage cases dealt with by the FMU in the given year
[b]In the Forced Marriage Unit's 2016 statistics, 54 other countries were represented in 109 (or 9%) of these cases. In addition, in 157 (or 11%) of the cases were identified as UK domestic only

Motivation for Forced Marriages

Forced marriage is caused by a number of factors. Any individual case may be motivated by one, some or all of the factors listed below. Motivations include[23]:

- a desire to protect the immediate and extended family's honour;
- a desire to protect children from negative cultural influences, for example, dressing in Westernised fashion, alcohol, sexual assault;
- to preserve cultural and/or religious traditions (however no major religion in the world condones or otherwise advocates forced marriage);

---

[23] HM Government Multi-agency practice guidelines, *Handling cases of Forced Marriage* (June 2014).

- to build stronger families;
- to strengthen family ties;
- to prevent unsuitable relationships, for example, marriage outside the caste system, culture or religion;
- to control sexual orientation and sexuality, for example, often lesbian, gay, bisexual or transgender people have been forced into marriages to 'cure' them or conceal their sexual orientation from family and community members;
- to retain wealth including land, property, financial wealth, within a family;
- to gain wealth, status and honour for the family;
- to honour agreements/contracts when the person(s) to be forced into the marriage were infants;
- in response to extended family and/or community pressure;
- to support and secure a spousal visa application to enter and stay in the UK;
- to prevent unsuitable relationships, for example, outside one's own faith group, religious sect, caste, etc.;
- to secure a carer for a child or adult with disabilities when the parent is unable to care for the person; and
- to protect girls at a time of war and conflict to avert sexual violence and the loss of honour.

It is noteworthy that the majority of these motives are related to appeals to cultural concerns, especially maintaining or enhancing social or community status, or maintaining cultural integrity, driven by a sense of maintaining or avoiding losing honour.

Warning Signs of Forced Marriage

There are a number of important warning signs of a forced marriage that professionals should be aware of. Certainly, the greater the number of these factors that are present for a case that is of concern, the more concerned professionals should be that forced marriage may be relevant to the case. These factors of course have to be considered with respect to the context of the situation in question, but where these occur professionals do need to set in train appropriate responses. These are discussed in the prevention section later in this chapter.

- Other siblings have previously undergone a forced marriage.
- A sibling has escaped the threat of a forced marriage.

- Victim and/or other siblings have gone missing (reported to police or not).
- Victim and/or siblings regularly go missing.
- Victim or other girl siblings have previously undergone female genital mutilation.
- The victim has been arrested for other reported offences, for example, shoplifting, substance misuse.
- Reports of domestic abuse, harassment, intimidation, threats etc. by family and/or community members.
- Self-harm or threats to self-harm.
- Reports of other crime, for example, kidnap, false imprisonment, sexual offences.
- Acid attack and other forms of physical assault.
- Victims and survivors trafficked into and/or across the UK.
- Unauthorised absence(s) from school during term time and irregular attendance.
- Fear about forthcoming holiday periods.
- Request for authorised absence and a failure to return to school.
- 'Policing' by siblings, extended family or community members.
- Decline in behaviour, punctuality and/or performance.
- Poor examination outcomes, especially if unexpected.
- Announcement of an engagement or proposal of marriage.
- Adult with support needs removed from day care centre.
- Accompanied to doctors or other medical appointments by family members.
- Self-harm/suicide attempts.
- Eating disorders.
- Depression/isolation.
- Substance misuse.
- Female genital mutilation.
- Social care previously involved with the person's family, for example, child subject to Police protection, Emergency Protection Order or Ward of Court due to risks presented by other family members.

Polygamous Marriages

Relevant to a discussion of forced marriage is also polygamous marriage. This is because individuals are often forced into polygamous marriages. It is important therefore to understand the characteristics of these marriages and the risks to victims/survivors, especially wives.

Polygamous marriages are unlawful in the UK (as they are in most Western democracies).

Polygamy is accepted in some cultural and religious groups, for example, the Church of Jesus Christ of Latter-Day Saints. Within the Islamic faith, according to some interpretations of the Qur'an, a man may have up to four wives at any one time. Shari'a law permits polygamy by allowing men to have two or more wives. However, polyandry, the practice of a woman having two or more husbands, is forbidden.

Polygamy is most common within rural communities, often because it provides help with agricultural work and to increase the likelihood of the conception of children. It is found most often in a number of geographical areas including North and West African countries, for example, Kenya, Senegal, Egypt, Sudan, Morocco, Yemen; and the Middle East, for example, Jordan, Syria, Iraq and amongst Israeli Bedouin.

However, there is evidence that wives within polygamous marriages are at high risk of abuse. They are likely to suffer threats of violence, coercive control and psychological abuse, and in some cases, physical and sexual assault. There is also a high risk of these wives being abandoned by husbands and becoming destitute, both with and without their children. Indeed, there is evidence that many hundreds of wives are abandoned by their UK-born bridegrooms in Asia and elsewhere annually. Often this happens after the wedding was accompanied by (in relative terms) a large dowry.[24]

As polygamous marriages are illegal in the UK, it is likely that any polygamous marriage in the UK is a consequence of an unregistered ceremony by a non-authorised celebrant. Also the parties of such marriages have no legal status and have no automatic entitlements should the other party die.[25] In addition, for abandoned wives who are foreign nationals there are other problems, for example, they may have no recourse to public funds to support their housing and other welfare needs. This can lead to spiralling poverty and disadvantage. The accompanying sense of shame for abandoned wives and their families can be overwhelming, exacerbated by the financial loss and the harmful negative views of other members of their communities.

---

[24] http://news.bbc.co.uk/1/hi/uk/8370459.stm accessed on 18 May 2016.
[25] Law Commission, *Getting Married, A Scoping Paper* (2015).

Sham Marriages or Marriages of Convenience

Also relevant to the issue of forced marriage are *sham marriage or marriages of convenience* (or sham civil partnerships). A sham marriage is a marriage that is conducted with the aim of obtaining a benefit by two people who are not a genuine couple. There is a clear distinction between a *classic sham marriage* and a *forced sham marriage*. In the case of the former, individuals freely enter into a criminal enterprise for money or other gain; this often results in an immigration advantage for one of the spouses. In the case of the latter, an individual is forced into a sham marriage with the intention that this will facilitate some benefit for the other party. A sham marriage should be distinguished from a consensual marriage entered into by a genuine couple where the marriage also affords benefits for the spouses such as for immigration or other reasons.[26]

Reports of suspected sham marriages by registration officials in the UK suggest that they are generally entered into by a non-European Economic Area (EEA) national and an EEA national or British Citizen. However, it is clearly possible for two non-EEA nationals to enter into a sham marriage. The UK Home Office estimates that following sham marriages there are 4000 to 10,000 applications per year to stay in the UK from individuals, either under the UK Immigration Rules or under the Immigration (EEA) Regulations 2006. The scale of this is suggestive of the involvement of organised criminal groups. Sham marriages organised by criminal groups are potentially very lucrative. For example, it has been reported that some individuals have paid up to £20,000 for a sham marriage to be facilitated.[27]

Human Trafficking

The links between sham marriage, forced marriage and human trafficking have been identified by the UK's National Crime Agency (NCA) and Europol.[28] The UK NCA reported that 11% of human trafficking cases in the UK in 2014 were trafficked solely for forced marriage. The majority of the cases involved Eastern European females trafficked into the UK to marry Asian men, who were not legally entitled to stay in the UK. Some of the trafficked victims and survivors reported being sexually exploited and being the

---

[26] Home Office, *Sham Marriages and Civil Partnership. Background Information and Proposed Referral and Investigation Scheme* (November 2013).

[27] Ibid.

[28] The National Crime Agency (NCA) is the UK's National Law Enforcement Agency, which was established in 2013.

victims and survivors of multiple forms of other forms of exploitation.[29] In March 2014, Europol issued an Early Warning notification to Member States after identifying an emerging trend of vulnerable European Economic Area (EEA) women being trafficked to be forced into sham marriages.[30] These cases can present challenges as law enforcement agencies have to distinguish trafficked victims and survivors from crime perpetrators falsely claiming this.

Annually in the UK, the number referred to the National Referral Mechanism (NRM) for Modern Slavery, that is, victims and survivors of Human Trafficking, Forced Labour and Domestic Servitude, continue to rise. In the period January–September 2019, there were 7273 referrals to the NRM, an increase of 45% compared to the same period in 2018. With victims and survivors most likely originating from Albania, Vietnam, China, Eritrea, India, Sudan, Romania, Nigeria and Pakistan. It appears that those engaged in organising modern slavery are most likely to operate in organised groups and are mostly likely to be men. However, the UK National Crime Agency (NCA) reports that the number of women engaged in organising modern slavery has increased and amounts to 34% of offenders. Where women are involved as offenders, it is most likely to be linked to sexual exploitation.[31]

Prevention

Forced Marriage: Criminal Offence in England and Wales

On 16 June 2014, the Anti-social Behaviour, Crime and Policing Act 2014 came into force, criminalising forced marriage.[32] The offences under this Act are punishable, depending on the mode of trial, by 12 months to 7 years of imprisonment. Section 121 of this law creates the offence of forced marriage in England and Wales and has been framed in a way that includes the typical methods used by perpetrators to affect their purpose of forcing the marriage, including violence, threats, coercion and deception.

---

[29] Ibid.

[30] Europol, Early Warning Notification, Marriages of convenience: A link between facilitation of illegal immigration and THB (Trafficking in Human Beings), (March 2014).

[31] NCA, National Strategic Assessment of Serious and Organised Crime, (2000), pp. 22–29 accessed via https://nationalcrimeagency.gov.uk/who-we-are/publications/437-national-strategic-assessment-of-serious-and-organised-crime-2020/file.

[32] http://www.legislation.gov.uk/ukpga/2014/12/section/121/enacted accessed on 23 July 2017.

The use of deception to lure a victim out of the UK to be forced into a marriage is specified in the legislation and included as this has been a regular modus operandi of forced marriages. It is not unusual for such deception to be on the pretext of visiting a sick or dying grandparent or other relative, family holiday or to attend someone else's wedding.

It is pertinent also that within the legislation, violence and threat of violence can be used towards any person in the process of forcing the marriage, and this does not necessarily have to be the individual who is going to be forced into marriage (Section 121 Sub-section 6 of the Act). In addition, this law has been framed to cover any type of marriage including religious and non-religious ceremonies whether or not they are legally binding.

The legislation is intended to be victim led, with the victim having the choice of whether to progress down a criminal or civil justice route, that is, obtaining a Forced Marriage (Civil Protection) Order (FMPO), following a threatened or actual forced marriage. However, the caveat to this is that, once a criminal case has been referred to the Crown Prosecution Service (CPS) for a decision to prosecute a perpetrator, the sole decision will be made by the CPS Prosecutor in accordance with the Director of Public Prosecution's (DPP) Guidance. That said, the prosecutor should always consider the victim's perspective as part of the Public Interest Test of their decision-making process. Similar provisions, although with minor deviations, are made under Section 122 of the same Act for offences in Scotland or individuals who have habitual residence in Scotland. The wording of Section 122 of the Act is the same as Section 121 although there are some exceptions.

A particular challenge for the legislation and in attempts to prevent forced marriage is the use of technology. According to the UK's Freedom Charity, some Imams in the UK have been conducting wedding ceremonies over the internet using Skype.[33] In one case, an 11-year-old home-educated girl from London was married on Skype to a 25-year-old man in Bangladesh.

Forced Marriage Protection Orders

Section 63C Forced Marriage (Civil Protection) Act 2007—Forced marriage protection orders, states a court may make an order for the purpose of protecting a person from being forced into a marriage or from any attempt to force someone into a marriage or protecting a person who has already been forced into a marriage. In deciding whether or not to grant an Order, a court

---

[33] https://www.easterneye.eu/skype-forced-marriage-growing-trend/ accessed on 23 July 2017.

must regard all the circumstances including the need to secure the health, safety and wellbeing of the person to be protected. The court should consider, so far as is practicable, the victim's wishes and feelings subject to their age and level of understanding.

In determining if force has been used to secure the marriage, as well as overt violence, coercion by threats or other psychological means must also be included. In granting an Order, the court may attach one or more conditions to the Order regarding the health, safety and wellbeing of the person to be protected. The court must attach a power of arrest to one or more provisions of the order unless it considers that, in all the circumstances of the case, there will be adequate protection without such a power.

Designated Family Law courts and the High Court may make an FMPO on an application being made by the person who is to be protected by the order, a relevant third party as determined by the Lord Chancellor, or any other person with the leave of the court such as the police service and civil society organisations.

The conditions attached to forced marriage protection orders may include:

- prevention of a forced marriage from occurring;
- parties to hand over all passports (including other passports held by dual nationals) and birth certificates and not to apply for a new passport;
- to stop intimidation, threats and violence;
- to reveal the whereabouts of a person;
- to stop someone from being taken abroad;
- to facilitate or enable a person to return to the UK within a given time period; and
- person to be produced at a British High Commission or British Embassy within a given time period;
- to prevent a person or persons from entering a specific geographic location.

The Anti-Social Behaviour, Crime and Policing Act 2014, Section 120 amended Part 4A Family Law Act 1996, introducing Section 63CA created a new offence of breaching a forced marriage protection order. This carries a maximum penalty of five years' imprisonment.

In England and Wales, the overall number of FMPO applications made to the 15 designated courts has remained relatively low, ranging from 20 to 100 per year, although there has been a gradual rise over time.[34] The authors argue

---

[34] Ministry of Justice, Family Court Statistics Quarterly, England and Wales, April to June 2019 (26.9.19) accessed via https://assets.publishing.service.gov.uk/government/uploads/system/uploads/attachment_data/file/834048/FCSQ_April_to_June_2019.pdf on 13 November 2019.

that it is crucial to monitor which agencies are applying for such orders to ensure that public authorities are discharging their safeguarding responsibilities. This would also provide an evidence base to allow more effective focusing of resources. It is critical that local authorities are fully conversant with obtaining FMPOs given the role that such orders play in safeguarding vulnerable people. Local authorities have a statutory role in safeguarding and protecting people.

There are similar provisions in Scotland for the granting of FMPOs to protect a person being forced into a marriage, or from attempting to force the person into a marriage or protecting someone who has already been forced into a marriage.[35]

Risk Management

As with the Section 121 offence, this legislation is intended to be victim led and the decision as to which course of action to take should be influenced by the victim or prospective victim. It is incumbent on the practitioner that they give victims/survivors an objective view of the legal position and to not pressurise them into making a decision. Such decisions will have lifelong implications for the individual. Practitioners should never lose sight of the fact that the risks to individuals increase once they approach the police, other statutory service providers or those in the legal sector. Such an approach will be seen as treacherous, dishonourable and bringing shame on both the victim and their family by both family member and other members of the affected community. As we have discussed in the HBA chapter, this brings risks of isolation, intimidation, harassment, physical assaults and threats to kill. It is also important to note that, for victims/survivors, the sense of isolation and fear can lead some to return to their abusive families and perpetrators.[36]

Given the above risks, obtaining FMPOs must never be seen as a so-called tick box exercise and the decision to make an application must be thoroughly risk assessed. An FMPO must not however be a standalone control measure. An FMPO should be complementary to a number of other risk management measures. Of particular concern is that during the FMU's 2008 review, it was found that police forces were not routinely informed of FMPOs that had powers of arrest attached to them, and that statutory agencies in most of the

---

[35] Section 1 Forced Marriage (Protection and Jurisdiction) (Scotland) Act 2011.

[36] HM Government, The Right to Choose: Multi-agency statutory guidance for dealing with forced marriage (2014), p. 9.

regions visited did not conduct any on-going monitoring of FMPOs once they had been granted.[37] This dearth of monitoring is also believed to be a factor in the lack of identification of breaches of FMPOs.[38] In the financial year 2018/2019, the CPS only prosecuted eight perpetrators for breaches of FMPOs; of which only three were convicted.[39]

We argue therefore that increased surveillance and monitoring of FMPOs is a key necessary step if more criminal breaches of orders are to be identified and prosecutions and convictions achieved. This however remains a key area of development for the police service, local authorities, education professionals and others who have a responsibility for protecting victims and survivors and the public. Additionally, the authors believe that adequate risk management and monitoring is a matter that touches on the trust and confidence of victims and survivors and the likelihood that they will report breaches to the police service.

As a necessary first step in more effectively monitoring FMPOs, it is essential that relevant third Parties and other applicants inform the police service of the granting of these orders. Once notified, the relevant police service must place the order's details on the police national computer and the police national (intelligence) database. In addition, the police service must also inform the UK Border Force and the UK Passport Authority when a travel restriction has been made.

The UK Forced Marriage Unit

The Forced Marriage Unit (FMU), which is a joint UK Foreign and Commonwealth Office and Home Office Unit, was set up in January 2005 to lead on the UK Government's forced marriage policy. It is the only unit of its kind in the world.[40] The unit operates both inside the UK and overseas.

The FMU provides protection for victims/survivors who have concerns about being forced into marriage. The assistance provided includes safety advice, assisting reluctant sponsors (a victim who wants to prevent their unwanted spouse, whom they have been forced to marry, moving to the UK), setting safety plans, and establishing safe communication methods with British nationals who have concerns about being forced into marriage before going on a family holiday or trip overseas. In some cases, assistance may even

---

[37] Home Office/Foreign and Commonwealth Office (FCO), Report On The Implementation Of The Multi-Agency Statutory Guidance For Dealing With Forced Marriage (2008), p. 24.

[38] Home Affairs Committee, *Eighth Report of Session 2010–12, Forced Marriage*, HC 880, para 9.

[39] CPS, Violence Against Women and Girls Report 2018–19, p. 20 https://www.cps.gov.uk/sites/default/files/documents/publications/cps-vawg-report-2019.pdf.

[40] https://www.gov.uk/guidance/forced-marriage#forced-marriage-unit.

involve mounting rescue operations with local law enforcement agencies to recover British nationals being held against their will. In addition to the above, the FMU also undertakes media campaigns and has an extensive outreach and awareness training programme focused on professionals and affected communities.

Successful UK Prosecutions

The first conviction in the UK for the criminal offence of forced marriage was secured in the South Wales police force area.[41] On 10 June 2015, a 34-year-old man from the South Wales area was sentenced to 16 years of imprisonment for crimes including forced marriage, rape, bigamy and voyeurism. The convicted man used duress by blackmailing his 25-year-old female victim using video footage of her showering and threatening to kill her family members, to force her to marry him. This was also an act of bigamy by him. The accused also repeatedly raped the victim. It is clear that the partnership of the police investigator, CPS and prosecuting counsel coupled with the victim's courage was an instrumental factor in securing the prosecution and conviction. Mr Iwan Jenkins, Head of CPS Wales Rape and Serious Sexual Offences Unit has said:

> It is a testament to the strength of the case which we constructed with the police that we secured a guilty plea for the offences in this case.[42]

In a more recent case, on 31 January 2020, a 55-year-old Birmingham man was sentenced to seven years of imprisonment after he tried to force his then 18-year-old niece into a marriage and for child cruelty offences. His 43-year-old wife was also found guilty of child neglect.

The victim was born in the UK and raised by her uncle and aunt in Birmingham after her mother returned to Pakistan due to an Immigration visa issue. She had been physically, psychologically and emotionally maltreated by the two. The girl was described as feeling like 'a nobody'. The victim was taken to Pakistan when she was ten where she lived in appalling conditions. She returned to the UK at age 14 to live with another family member where she completed her education and went on to get a job.

---

[41] As defined by the Anti-Social Behaviour Crime and Policing Act 2015, Section 121.

[42] http://www.cps.gov.uk/news/latest_news/uk_s_first_forced_marriage_conviction/ accessed on 27 August 2017.

In July 2016, the victim travelled to Pakistan to visit her sick mother. When the teenager arrived in Pakistan, her uncle seized her passport and kept her at his house where he tried to force her into a marriage. When she tried to refuse, he threatened her with a gun and told her to either get married to a husband of his choosing or die.

She later escaped Pakistan with the support of a friend who had smuggled a mobile telephone to her. The victim called the British Embassy for help and in September 2017, she was rescued and repatriated to the UK. Upon arriving back in the UK, a Forced Marriage Prevention Order (FMPO) was issued for her protection.[43]

Summary and Recommendations

Forced marriage is a global problem requiring a consistent and resilient transnational action plan to combat it. There are many international Conventions and Articles and national legislation that are designed to combat it, yet the levels of forced marriage (and child forced marriage, see next chapter) remain significant. This will see many children and young people married against their will leading to a fundamental denial of their human rights and serious crimes being committed against them.

In the UK we do not know the true prevalence of forced marriage as different agencies rely upon different datasets. This inconsistent approach is in itself leading to uncoordinated action being taken and is hampering the efficient prioritisation of resources. It is of the upmost importance that government and other agencies work together with communities to empower them to identify and implement sustainable solutions to eradicate forced marriage. It is also essential to raise awareness amongst professionals—police officers, health workers, social workers and teachers as well as employers and affected communities of the warning signs of forced marriage, so that they may be more empowered to make timely interventions to prevent crimes and to safeguard and protect lives.

Whilst prosecutions and convictions have taken place, it is of notable concern that the number of prosecutions and convictions for forced marriage are declining in England Wales. The CPS report that in the financial year 2018–2019, there were four offences of forced marriage charged/prosecuted

---

[43] https://www.cps.gov.uk/west-midlands/news/birmingham-man-jailed-trying-force-niece-marriage accessed 31 January 2020.

and three of the four defendants were convicted. This is substantially less from previous years whereby 2016–2017 saw 44 prosecutions followed by 50 prosecutions the years after.[44,45]

The CPS and the police are working together to improve the quality of investigations and prosecution performance, which includes the development of a joint police/CPS stakeholder group, updates to CPS's guidance and the implementation of a quality assurance process to review the flagging of forced marriage cases. In addition, there are joint conferences to identify good practice and lessons learnt.

However, crucial to this, is that any scrutiny process must be underpinned by independence, accountability and subject matter expertise. It is also crucial that specialist NGOs and subject matter experts are involved in the aforementioned processes to add further informed value.

---

[44] CPS, Violence against Women and Girls Report 2018–19, pp. 19 and 20 https://www.cps.gov.uk/sites/default/files/documents/publications/cps-vawg-report-2019.pdf.

[45] CPS, Violence against Women and Girls Report 2017–18, p. 13 https://www.cps.gov.uk/sites/default/files/documents/publications/cps-vawg-report-2018.pdf.

5

Child and Early Forced Marriage

In this chapter, we explore forced marriage of children and adolescents, so-called child and early forced marriage (CEFM). Many of the issues relevant to CEFM are those raised in the previous chapter on forced marriage, so this chapter needs to be read in conjunction with the previous chapter. However, there are some important issues that are specific to CEFM upon which we concentrate here. We will define what is meant by CEFM, explore the worldwide prevalence, consider legislative approaches and identify reasons why CEFM occurs. Finally, we will identify warning signs of CEFM that may enable early identification by professionals and others charged with safeguarding children. In this chapter, we hope to illustrate that CEFM is a form of child abuse and a gross breach of girls' and boys' human rights.[1]

Definition

Child or early marriage is defined with respect to the age at which a child becomes an adult. In the UK and in many other countries, a child is defined as any person under the age of 18 years.[2] This is further reinforced by Article 1 of The Convention on the Rights of the Child,[3] which defines a child as

---

[1] The minimum age at which a person is able to consent to a marriage is 16 years old; however, a person under the age of 18 can marry in England and Wales with parental consent unless that person is a widow/widower as per the Matrimonial Causes Act 1973 Section 11(a)(ii).

In Scotland, people can marry at 16 years without parental consent.

[2] Children's Act 2008 and Children & Young Persons Act 1989.

[3] http://ohchr.org/EN/ProfessionalInterest/Pages/CRC.aspx accessed on 28 July 2017.

© The Author(s) 2020
G. Campbell et al., *Harmful Traditional Practices*,
https://doi.org/10.1057/978-1-137-53312-8_5

every human being below the age of eighteen years unless under the law applicable to the child, majority is attained earlier.

Thus, any marriage that occurs when one or both of the protagonists is aged prior to 18 falls within the realm of CEFM.

The age of those married is particularly important relative to a jurisdiction's age of consent. Where individuals are married and they are younger than the official age of consent, even if the marriage has parental consent, we should consider this a forced marriage. This is because, in these circumstances, the children of the marriage cannot be legally said to have given informed consent to the marriage.

Prevalence

It is estimated that 900 million people or 13% of the world's population have been affected by CEFM. There are 720 million women in the world who were married before their 18th birthday, every year 15 million girls are married before the age of 18 years and 250 million were married before their 15th birthdays.[4] This translates to one in nine girls being married before the age of 15, with some child brides as young as five years old. Relatedly, according to UNICEF, 156 million men worldwide were married before their 18th birthday, and 33 million were married before their 15th birthdays.[5]

Worldwide, nations with the highest rates of child marriage before the age of 18 are shown in Table 5.1.[6] As can be seen, the countries with the highest percentage of CEFM are situated on the African continent. According to the UNICEF, the total number of child brides in Africa will be likely to more than double over the next 35 years, rising from 125 million to 310 million.[7] It is estimated that by 2050, Africa will surpass South Asia as the region with the highest number of women aged 20 to 24 who were married as children.

However, we must be clear CEFM is not just a problem for African nations. CEFM exists in many other countries too including the UK and USA. The statistics produced by the Office for National Statistics for 2012–2018, show that in this period 585 males and 2770 females aged 16 or 17 were married in

---

[4] http://www.girlsnotbrides.org/wp-content/uploads/2014/10/GNB-factsheet-on-child-marriage-numbers-Oct-2014.pdf accessed on 28 July 2017.

[5] UNICEF, Ending Child Marriage, Progress and Prospects, 2014.

[6] https://data.unicef.org/topic/child-protection/child-marriage accessed on 1 March 2017.

[7] United Nations Children's Fund, *A Profile of Child Marriage in Africa*, UNICEF, New York, 2015.

Table 5.1 Nations with the highest rates of child marriage

Ranking	Country	Underaged/Child/Forced 'Marriage' Under 18 years
1	Niger	76%
2	Central African Republic	68%
2	Chad	68%
3	Bangladesh	65%
4	Mali	55%
5	Burkina Faso	52%
5	Guinea	52%
5	South Sudan	52%
6	Malawi	50%
7	Mozambique	48%
7	India	47%
8	Somalia	45%
9	Sierra Leone	43%
10	Nigeria	42%

the UK.[8] For both sexes a higher proportion were married when they were 17 years old. There were no official cases recorded of marriage registered for under 16 years in the UK. This is perhaps not surprising given that across the UK those age under 16 are not legally permitted to marry (see previous chapter on forced marriage for laws relevant to the legal age of marriage).[9] However, it appears that contrary to these data, child marriages do occur in the UK. The UK government's Forced Marriage Unit (FMU) statistics (see Table 5.2) highlight that there were child marriages within the UK, with between 13 and 18% of those seeking help from the FMU with concerns about forced marriage being under 16 years old. Indeed, one of the youngest cases of a CEFM managed by the Forced Marriage Unit was recorded in 2011 and related to a five-year-old girl.[10] A year later, the FMU managed a case involving a two-year-old child.[11] Similarly, NGOs, such as the UK's Freedom Charity, Karma Nirvana and the Iranian & Kurdish Women's Rights Organisation (IKWRO) also report cases involving children under the age of 12 years.

In the USA, there are also a large number of cases of child and early marriage, often despite legislation designed to outlaw it. A study by the

[8] Office for National Statistics, Marriages in England Wales (28 March 2019) accessed via https://www.ons.gov.uk/peoplepopulationandcommunity/birthsdeathsandmarriages/marriagecohabitationandcivilpartnerships/datasets/marriagesinenglandandwales2013 on 12 October 2019.
[9] Ibid.
[10] Ibid.
[11] https://www.gov.uk/government/uploads/system/uploads/attachment_data/file/141823/Stats_2012.pdf accessed on 13 August 2017.

Table 5.2   UK Forced Marriage Unit figures for number of forced marriages and proportion involving children and adolescents[a]

Year	Nos. of cases	% under 16 years old	% 16–17 years old	Total % under 18 years old
2012	1485	13	22	35
2013	1302	15	25	40
2014	1267	11	11	22
2015	1220	14	13	27
2016	1428	15	11	26
2017	1196	15.6	14.1	29.7
2018	1764	17.7	14.9	32.6

[a]Foreign & Commonwealth Office and Home Office, Guidance Forced Marriage accessed via https://www.gov.uk/guidance/forced-marriage accessed on 1 March 2016

not-for-profit organisation, Unchained at Last, found that between the years 2000 and 2010, 248,000 children under 18 were married in the USA, with more young girls married than boys.[12] In a number of the US States reporting data for the study, the youngest child married was 14 years old and there were cases of younger children identified. This despite the fact that all US States have a law that a child, that is, a person under 18 years cannot marry without parental consent, or judicial authority if they are younger than 16 years.

A study by the US-based Tahirih Justice Centre found that in 27 states there are no laws stipulating the minimum age for marriage if the marriage is approved by a judge.[13] Furthermore, even in states where minimum ages are stipulated, in some cases this serves to legalise marriage between children. For example, case law in Massachusetts directs that males must be at least age 14 and females must be at least age 12 to marry.[14] The aforementioned study also identified nine US States that had statutes permitting the marriage of boys and girls between the ages of 13 and 15 years.

Motivation

The motivations for CEFM are complex, interrelated and similar to those affecting adults who are forced into marriage. Factors can include[15]:

[12] http://www.unchainedatlast.org/laws-to-end-child-marriage/ accessed on 12 June 2017.

[13] http://www.tahirih.org/news/statutory-compilation-shows-how-state-laws-permit-child-marriage-to-persist-in-present-day-america/ accessed on 12 June 2017.

[14] http://www.tahirih.org/wp-content/uploads/2016/11/FINAL-State-Marriage-Age-Requirements-Statutory-Compilation-PDF.pdf accessed on 13 June 2017.

[15] The UN Secretary General's in-depth study of all forms of violence against women, A/61/122/Add.1, (2006), Section IV, p. 36.

- Gender and social inequality.
- Poverty and insecurity.
- Retaining wealth within families.
- Social pressure and a desire to conform to traditional values.
- Preservation and maintenance of family honour.
- Failure to enforce local and international laws.
- Conflicts and disasters (can be linked to poverty and security).
- Dispute resolution between families, clans etc. where girls are traded as property.

Like all of the harmful traditional practices considered in this book, CEFM is often associated with concerns about family honour, and violent assaults can occur as a result of a child refusing to accept or attempting to escape or otherwise resist a marriage. This is illustrated in the case study of Bea, below (see also the chapter on honour-based abuse in this book).

> **Case Study: Bea 14 Years Old[16]**
>
> Bea, a 14-year-old Kenyan girl, was forced to undergo FGM during the school holidays. She was going to be forced to marry a 67-year-old man after her parents sold her for 2 kgs of tea leaves and 10 kgs of sugar, her bride price. Not unsurprising Bea was terrified and had a screaming fit on the day her intended husband came to collect her, screaming that she would not go with him and would not marry him. The older man left after some time telling Bea's father that when she calmed down, he would return for her.
>
> When Bea's intended husband left the homestead, her father felt ashamed and angered because Bea had dishonoured him by disobeying him and refusing to marry. Bea's punishment for not listening to him was that her brothers pinned her to the ground and her father cut off her ear lobes with a machete. Once her wounds had healed, Bea was forced to marry the 67-year-old man. Bea was subsequently rescued and is safely residing in a rescue centre alongside a large number of girls who faced similar fates.

Effects of CEFM

CEFM has a number of pernicious effects that apply to individuals, their families and whole communities. These include deep and lifelong physical and psychological injuries as a result of physical, emotional and sexual abuse.

---

[16] Bea is a pseudonym given to this victim to protect her identity.

According to research carried out by the World Health Organisation, married girls aged between 15 to 19 years are more likely to experience violence, including physical, sexual and emotional abuse, than older married women. There is an increased risk of mortality both through physical abuse and early (and dangerous) pregnancy. Victims and survivors of CEFM typically have children very young. However, girls under 15 are 5 times more likely to die in childbirth than women in their 20s and face higher risk of pregnancy-related injuries, such as obstetric fistula. Indeed, approximately 70,000 girls die in labour every year because their bodies aren't ready for childbirth. Finally, especially in the case of young girls, CEFM means that children do not get opportunities for education. This in turn severely limits their future economic opportunities, leading to a cycle of poverty both for the individual, their family and the community more broadly.

Prevention

National and International Law

We refer the reader to the previous chapter on forced marriage for a more detailed discussion of relevant legislation and laws surrounding marriage and specific provision surrounding forced marriage. The legislative approaches towards forced marriage are applicable for CEFM. Here we concern ourselves with issues specific to CEFM.

The international community, through the United Nations (UN), has agreed on a number of Declarations, which were intended to set universal equality and other standards.[17] Under the Convention on the Rights of the Child (CRC), governments have committed to ensure the overall protection of children and young people aged under 18. The Convention on the Elimination of All Forms of Discrimination against Women (CEDAW) consists of 30 articles and was adopted in 1979 by the UN General Assembly. Over 50 countries have ratified the Convention. Of interest to the present discussion is Article 16 that provides 'the betrothal and the marriage of a child shall have no legal effect',[18] essentially rendering all child marriages illegal under international conventions.

---

[17] http://www.un.org/womenwatch/daw/cedaw/ accessed on 28 July 2017.
[18] Ibid.

In 1999, the African Union developed the African Charter on the Rights and Welfare of the Child relating to children under 18 years.[19] The Charter recognises what it describes as the,

unique and privileged position that children have in African society and ... the child should grow up in a family environment in an atmosphere of happiness, love and understanding.[20]

The Charter also recognises that the mental and physical health and the social development of the child requires legal protection, particularly as it relates to freedom, dignity and security. Alongside this recognition, there are 48 Articles protecting the rights of the child. Of pertinent note is Article 1 of the Charter, which relates to the 'Obligation of States' Parties'. The third point of this article states that,

Any custom, tradition, cultural or religious practice that is inconsistent with the rights, duties and obligations contained in the present Charter shall to the extent of such inconsistency be discouraged.[21]

Despite all of this and the fact that in many countries throughout the world child marriage is explicitly prohibited, as we have seen it continues. This is because in many jurisdictions statutory laws are either not enforced, provide exceptions for parental/guardian consent,[22] or local customary law is used in deference to the statutory provisions. Given this state of affairs, parents, as the principal perpetrators of forced marriages, may be likely to give consent to a marriage even where their child did not or could not consent, or may use other legal instruments such as a judge's consent to force the marriage.

As we saw in the previous chapter, there is considerable variation in legislation leading to opportunities for CEFM. In the UK it is legal to get married in England, Wales and Ireland from 16 years old subject to parental consent, whereas in Scotland at 16 individuals can marry without parental consent.[23] In the USA, some states have legislation that, whilst broadly outlawing child

---

[19] http://www.un.org/womenwatch/daw/cedaw/text/econvention.htm accessed on 7 February 2017.

[20] Ibid.

[21] Ibid.

[22] As is the case in Scotland where consenting parties can be married at 16 years (without parent consent). In England and Wales, parties 16 and over but 18 years can be married with parental consent.

[23] Marriage Acts 1949 1994, Matrimonial Causes Act 1973 (for England Wales) and Marriage (Scotland) Act 1977.

marriage, because there is often no lower age on marriages that can be approved by a judge, they effectively legalise CEFM. In some developing countries, marriageable age varies according to gender. For example, in Bangladesh 18 years for females and 21 years for males, Pakistan 16 years for females and 18 years for males, Egypt 16 years for females and 18 years for males, Gambia 21 years for both females and males, or parental consent if below this age.

In some Muslim majority countries, the consent of a walayat-al-jabr or wali (marriage guardian) must also be given before a marriage can take place. Most commonly, the wali is an individual's father or grandfather. Here consent may follow national legislation or may, for many reasons, especially the particular needs of the respective families, be ignored. In some countries, such as Algeria, Malaysia and Sri Lanka, if a wali unreasonably withholds consent then the parties may resort to the courts to obtain permission.[24]

In some regions, common practice exists that effectively allows child marriage. For example, the marriageable age for girls is 10 or the attainment of puberty in Kano and Sokoto States in Nigeria.

Where legislation is ignored throughout the world, or where legislation permits child marriage with low age of consent rules, this is a reflection that child marriage is a deeply ingrained cultural practice. This means that despite all of the legislation and international agreements, eradication of this practice, like many other harmful traditional practices, can only be brought about by community-driven solutions.[25]

Warning Signs of CEFM

There are a number of warning signs for CEFM. The reader is directed to the chapter on Forced Marriage for a list of these. The reader is also referred to the section in that chapter on risk management as many of the points raised there are applicable to CEFM. The early identification of the warning signs is a key facet in providing timely effective support to the girls and boys at risk of CEFM to protect and safeguarding them.

As many of the victims and survivors of CEFM are children, it is education services that may be the first to identify the warning signs of an impending forced marriage. Indeed, teachers may be among the first persons to whom a

---

[24] Women Living Under Muslim Laws, *Knowing our Rights: Women, family, laws and customs in the Muslim World* (Russell Press, 2006).

[25] The UN Secretary General's in-depth study of all forms of violence against women, A/61/122/Add.1, (2006), para, p. 30.

child discloses their fear of CEFM. For many children, schools and other places of education offer a safe environment and escape from the fear and isolation that they face at home. However, potential victims and survivors may be 'policed' or otherwise surveilled by male siblings, cousins and/or community members who will report back their movements and behaviour to parents and other family members, for example, what they were doing, who they were speaking to and so on. The cumulative effect of such fear can have a destructive effect on individuals resulting in declining attendance, declining performance and declining behaviour. This may also lead to various health implications highlighted.

Similar to performance, school attendance is also affected. The lack of attendance at school and unauthorised or overdue absences from school, particularly (but not exclusively) before the summer holiday period, are important warning signs of potential victimisation.[26] In the past, perpetrators' modus operandi (MO) have included victims and survivors leaving the UK on the pretext of visiting a sick grandparent or going on a family holiday. This is used with such frequency that it was included as a specific element of the UK criminal offence of forced marriage, as discussed in the previous chapter.[27] Indeed, in its statutory guidance for local authorities, the UK Department for Education sets out safeguarding responsibilities that schools should track any absences or failure to return after holiday periods and investigate any unexplained absences of its pupils.[28] Given that there is a heightened risks during the summer holidays the UK Forced Marriage Unit issued an advisory warning before in 2012, which stated[29]:

> *Summer holidays are the peak time for young people to be taken overseas and forced into a marriage against their will. In some cases, they are taken on what they have been told is a holiday to visit family abroad, but in fact a marriage has been planned. Once abroad, victims and survivors are often even more isolated than they might have been in the UK and getting help is more difficult.*

Healthcare professionals have a similar role in tackling CEFM. As with teachers, healthcare professionals may also be among the first to whom potential victims and survivors may disclose their situation or may show health effects of abuse consistent with CEFM.

---

[26] https://www.gov.uk/government/news/forced-marriage-warning-as-summer-holidays-approach accessed on 13 August 2017.

[27] Antisocial Behaviour Crime and Police Act 2014, Section 121.

[28] Education Act 2002, Section 175.

[29] https://www.gov.uk/government/news/forced-marriage-warning-as-summer-holidays-approach accessed on 13 August 2017.

Children's social care has a significant role to play in tackling and preventing CEFM. Children with or without support needs are especially vulnerable to the threat of being forced into a marriage.

Summary and Recommendations

CEFM is a crime throughout the world and represents a gross breach of the human rights of children. Girls are predominately the victims and survivors of this abuse, its perpetration deeply rooted in gender inequality. The effects of CEFM are an absence of education, employment and other economic opportunities for victims and survivors and a high risk of violence, abuse and discrimination. In addition, CEFM results in significant health problems for its victims and survivors as a result of early pregnancy in girls and other forms of physical and psychological abuse.

Despite many public policies and declarations condemning the practice of CEFM, loopholes in law or explicit legislation permitting CEFM, allows the practice to continue. Loopholes and supportive legislation must be ended if CEFM is to be eradicated. We recognise that whilst strategies, policies and action plans are important, they will not by themselves eradicate CEFM. To achieve sustainable and lasting change, as we have noted repeatedly in this book, affected communities must also want to change and end this harmful practice. They must also be supported and empowered to do so. To this end, it is of the upmost importance that governments, public authorities and civil society organisations work together with communities to empower them to identify and implement sustainable solutions to eradicate CEFM. This support should come in the form of education and awareness raising of the serious health impacts for a child or young person and the longer-term socio-economic consequences, which disempower individuals, families and communities. CEFM imprisons girls in particular and gives them a life sentence enduring the highly negative consequences of such gender inequality and discrimination.

We must not overlook the fact that CEFM is also a 'first world' problem affecting the UK, USA, Australia and European countries. It is essential therefore that, in addition to other professionals involved in safeguarding children, registrars of marriages and other authorised marriage celebrants and their staff receive training so that they can recognise the warning signs of forced marriage and CEFM and take action where it is appropriate to do so. Indeed, registrars and assistant registrars of marriages and other duly authorised marriage celebrants are the last line of defence for CEFM victims and survivors and have a professional and a moral responsibility to prevent such marriages from taking place.

To conclude, CEFM is preventable and education and action by professionals and others is fundamental to its prevention. Children must be enabled through education to make autonomous decisions and be empowered to realise their full potential in life.

6

Breast Ironing

Breast 'ironing', also known as breast 'flattening' and breast 'whipping' (although there are other regional variations in the terms used) is a harmful traditional practice that involves the mutilation of a girl's breasts with the aim of flattening the growing breasts of pre-pubescent or pubescent girls. Breast ironing is conducted because it is believed by those practicing it that it prevents unwelcome male attention by delaying signs of sexual maturity in young girls. It is believed further that this 'protects' the victim from unwanted events such as sexual harassment, sexual assault or pregnancy.

Little is currently known about breast ironing especially among frontline professionals who are charged with protecting children and are most likely to encounter victims and survivors. Indeed, it has not been the subject of minimal research and consideration within academia or among professionals. This was illustrated in a recent debate in the UK's Parliament. In calling for breast ironing to be made a specific criminal offence, Jake Berry MP reported his concern about the 'lack of hard facts and figures'. He illustrated this by reporting responses he had received from United Kingdom Police forces and Local Government Authorities to questions he posed to them about their knowledge and experience of breast ironing. He stated,

> *The police forces that wrote back to me showed real concern. They know that this is a worrying crime and they have a worrying lack of knowledge of it. Some 72% of the police forces that responded either failed to answer a question about breast ironing or admitted that they had never heard of it, while 38% said they wanted more guidance. This demonstrates a lack of understanding among our police forces about breast ironing and the signs that reveal that it is happening....*

© The Author(s) 2020
G. Campbell et al., *Harmful Traditional Practices*,
https://doi.org/10.1057/978-1-137-53312-8_6

He also noted that Local Authorities were in a similar state of uncertainty, requiring significantly more information and training on the subject. He stated,

> Of those who responded, 23% volunteered the information that they had never undertaken any training in this area, and 65% said that they would like more guidance.

Given the need for greater awareness, this chapter explores the characteristics of breast ironing, its origins, prevalence, motivation, effects upon victims and survivors and methods of prevention.

Definition

There is no universally accepted definition of breast ironing as there is scant literature on the subject. As noted, breast ironing has a number of other labels, including breast flattening and breast whipping, as well as a range of other regional labels. For clarity, we will use the term breast ironing. We urge others to use this term as well. This is so that victims and survivors, community groups and other professionals exposed to harmful traditional practices have a common vocabulary. For clarity we also provide an operational definition of breast ironing that accords with the majority of other definitions available. We therefore formally define breast ironing as the mutilation of (usually) a young girl's breast, using a wide range of procedures that have the aim of flattening the breasts.

Methods of Breast Ironing

Breast ironing is most commonly carried out by pressing, pounding or massaging the breasts with heated objects such as stones, spatulas or wooden paddles. Other methods used include a belt to tie or bind the breasts flat (this method has been found among some richer families in Cameroon), and/or the application of leaves thought to have special medicinal or healing qualities, plantain peels, stones, fruit pits, coconut shells, salt, ice or napkins. This typically starts at the first appearance of a young girl's breasts. The frequency of treatment varies with some reports of a single treatment of heated leaves placed ceremonially on the breasts, others reports describe treatment occurring twice a day for weeks or months to crush the knot of the budding breast.[1]

Motivation

The motivation for breast ironing appears to be related to concerns about personal and familial honour (see the chapter on HBA in this book). To recap that discussion, in cultures that place a high value on honour, a female's honour (and often that of her family) is measured and maintained by her behaviour. Honour is lost when the female behaves in an 'unacceptable' manner, in particular in a way perceived to be sexually promiscuous. Within this belief system, any form of male attention directed towards a young girl, whether invited by her or not, is regarded as unwanted as it may make the girl *appear* to be sexually promiscuous. This produces dishonour and shame for the girl and her family. Taking steps to reduce the risk of male attention therefore serves to reduce the risk of dishonour and shame. Among affected communities, reducing or removing signs of developing sexual maturity, such as 'ironing the breast', is one method of reducing the risk of male attention and so 'protecting' the honour of daughters.

As with other activities associated with familial honour described in this book, being known or seen to have engaged in breast ironing by other community members who are supportive of this practice, can help maintain and enhance a family's honour, publicly demonstrating that the family 'cares' for their daughter and their own honour.

The relationship with honour concerns is further highlighted by the observation that girls who have not undergone breast ironing can also be dishonoured and shamed. In essence they and their family have failed to take all necessary steps to preserve the girl's honour. This can result in social isolation, stigmatisation and false accusations about the girl's perceived sexual promiscuity, and the family's lack of concern for community values, tradition and standards.

As well as appeals to honour and tradition, it is important to note that some mothers engage in the practice for reasons that they considered may be helpful to their daughter. Some mothers may support breast ironing because removal of signs of puberty can mean that her daughter in some cultures can pursue education for longer rather than being regarded as 'ready for marriage'.

---

[1] https://www.academia.edu/12252029/Understanding_Breast_Ironing_A_study_of_the_methods_motivations_and_outcomes_of_breast_flattening_practices_in_Cameroon.

In these circumstances, the girl might also come to believe that what her mother is doing is for her own good. This is important for professionals to bear in mind as this may have a significant impact upon the willingness of the girl to report her victimisation or to support attempts at prosecution.

Origins

Breast ironing is believed to have originated in West Africa, especially Cameroon, although similar customs have been documented in Togo, the Republic of Guinea, South Africa and Côte d'Ivoire. In common with other harmful traditional practices, breast ironing also takes place in nations within the global North, particularly among the West African diaspora.[2]

Prevalence

The UN estimates that some 3.8 million teenage girls are affected by breast ironing and has identified breast 'ironing' as one of the five forgotten crimes against women.[3] In the UK, although there is currently no data on prevalence, CAME Women and Girls Development Organisation (CAWOGIDO) estimates that 1000 girls are at risk of or have been subject to breast ironing. Cases have been reported in London, Yorkshire, Essex and the West Midlands area, and an unknown number have occurred overseas.[4] Given that this offence is frequently carried out under conditions of high secrecy, these estimates are likely to significantly underestimate the true prevalence.

Perpetrators

Mothers appear to be the most likely perpetrators of breast ironing. A study by the Cameroon Department of Public Health Sciences found that the majority of perpetrators were female relatives of the victim: 58% of the practice was undertaken by a victim's mother, 10% by a nanny, 9% by a sister and 7% by a grandmother. There is also evidence that it can be performed by a

---

[2] More information about CAME Women and Girls can be found by visiting http://cawogido.co.uk/our-organisation/.

[3] https://www.unfpa.org/press/violence-against-women-stories-you-rarely-hear-about.

[4] https://hansard.parliament.uk/Commons/2016-03-22/debates/16032252000002/BreastIroning accessed on 19 August 2017.

nurse, caretaker, aunt, older sister, grandmother or the victim herself. In a minority of cases the perpetrator was a traditional healer, father or other family member, friends or neighbours. It has been noted that the father and other male family members often remain completely unaware of this practice. However, as with other forms of harmful traditional practice, this may be more a case of men overlooking or ignoring the practice. Men often believed that it is 'women's work' to bring up and educate children, particularly girls.

Victim Characteristics

The risk of undergoing breast ironing appears to depend upon the age when the breasts first appear. In the aforementioned study in Cameroon: for girls whose breasts develop before the age of 9, there is a 50% chance of having the breasts 'ironed'. The rate is 38% for girls whose breasts grew before 11, 24% for girls whose breasts grew before 12 years of age and 14% for girls whose breasts grew before the age of 14. The Cameroon study also found that 70% of the breasts were bandaged or attached with breast bands after the 'ironing' while 30% used under-sized breast wear.[5]

Effects of Breast Ironing

Breast ironing takes a significant physical and psychological toll on victims and survivors. As well as being extremely painful during the 'ironing' procedures, it also exposes girls to physical health problems including abscesses, cysts, various infections, tissue damage, and even the disappearance of one or both breasts. For example, according to the Cameroon study described above, a plethora of negative health effects were reported among them[6]:

- Severe pain,
- high fever,
- abscess in the breast,
- breasts pimples on and around the nipples,
- cysts in the breasts,
- itching of breasts,

---

[5] Department of Public Health Sciences: Breast Ironing in Cameroon: Just a Rumour? Mancho Innocent Ndifor, Karolinska Institutet, Master theses in Public Health; Board of Education in Public Health Sciences at Karolinska Institutet.

[6] UNICEF Behind Closed Doors https://www.unicef.org/media/files/BehindClosedDoors.pdf accessed 2 February 2020

- severe chest pain,
- flow of breasts,
- milk infection of breasts as a result of scarification,
- one breast being bigger than the other,
- breasts not increasing in size,
- disappearance of the breasts.

In addition, ten cases of breast cancer were identified in women who underwent breast ironing.[7] There are also significant psychological affects including depression, anxiety, fear of parents and issues with trust. Alongside the physical effects of breast ironing, the psychological effects are often associated with chronic health consequences.

Prevention

Many of the issues concerned with how to prevent and respond to breast ironing are similar to those concerning the other harmful cultural practices considered in this book. Hence, in this section we will consider issues that are specific to breast ironing.

Legislation

To the knowledge of the authors, there is no legislation in any jurisdiction that specifically tackles breast ironing, nor does there appear to be any sentencing guideline that recognise the role that this harmful traditional practice plays in controlling the sexuality and the sexual autonomy of girls.

Due to the lack of a standalone crime of breast ironing, police and prosecutors have to rely upon the existing pool of criminal offences available to them. In the UK as in other jurisdictions, the police have a range of other arrestable offences at their disposal to deal with any cases that they encounter; this includes common assault, actual bodily harm or grievous bodily harm, child cruelty and causing or allowing a child to suffer serious physical harm as well as various sexual offences.

In the UK, for example, breast ironing is most likely to be a crime contrary to the Offences Against the Persons Act, although this act does not specifically

---

[7]HMIC, The Depths of dishonour: Hidden voices and shameful crimes (December 2015) para. 8.13, p. 76 accessed via https://www.justiceinspectorates.gov.uk/hmicfrs/wp-content/uploads/the-depths-of-dishonour.pdf.

include discussion of breast ironing. To date, this legislation has not been tested in this respect, indeed there has been only one case of breast ironing reported to the police in the UK, in London, which did not progress to a prosecution. There have been no prosecutions for offences related to breast ironing either elsewhere in the UK or indeed in any other Western democracy.

In addition, the physical and psychological injuries caused or inflicted on children under 18 years of age amount to significant harm under the United Kingdom Children Act 1989, thereby triggering safeguarding and child protection procedures in the event of detection of this offending.[8]

Partnership Responses

As we make clear throughout this book, as with all of the harmful traditional practices, there is a need for a collaborative justice approach where the focus is on prevention. This is best served by raising awareness of the characteristics of the practice, among police, teachers, health and social care professionals. In addition, these professions and other relevant organisations need to work together and in partnership with affected communities.[9,10]

All public authorities must adopt a proactive approach to engaging with affected communities, raising awareness and developing confidence and trust to encourage victims and survivors to come forward.[11] In addition to securing confidence and trust, community engagement may also secure intelligence from communities on who is perpetrating this practice, where and how it is practiced as well as other harmful practices.

Give the above, there is an urgent need to ensure that all professionals are provided with statutory guidance on how to effectively identify and manage cases of breast ironing, including how it can present. Indeed, all professionals have a key role to play in identifying, preventing and tackling this harmful

---

[8] Significant Harm—The Children Act 1989 introduced the concept of 'significant harm' as the threshold that justifies compulsory intervention in family life in the best interests of children and young people. Harm is defined in Section 31(9), Children Act 1989, whilst Section 31(10) provides limited guidance as to what will be considered significant harm. Local authorities have a duty to make enquiries to decide whether they should take action to safeguard or promote the welfare of a child who is suffering, or likely to suffer, significant harm under Section 47 of the Children Act 1989. The definition of harm in Section 31(9) was amended by the Adoption and Children Act 2002 to include, "for example, impairment suffered from seeing or hearing the ill-treatment of another".

[9] HM Government, Working together to safeguard children, March 2015 accessed on 18 August 2017 via www.gov.uk/government/publications/working-together-to-safeguard-children%2D%2D2.

[10] Welsh Assembly Government, Safeguarding Children: Working Together Under the Children Act 2004, (2006) accessed on 18 August 2017 via www.gov.wales/topics/health/publications/socialcare/circular/nafwc1207/?lang=enf Section 47(1)(a)(ii) of the Children Act 1989.

[11] HMIC, HBA inspection. HMIC (2015). The depths of dishonour: Hidden voices and shameful crimes.

practice using their existing statutory safeguarding responsibilities to protect girls at risk or those who have already been offended against.[12,13]

For those who have already been subjected to breast ironing, the role of health professionals is key to identifying them. Indeed, such women are likely to be suffering long-term problems with breast health or may be experiencing difficulty breast feeding. In this regard, it is likely that breast screening and maternity services are among the most effective ways of providing early identification of victims and survivors. Familiarity with breast ironing, the practice and its consequences are therefore crucial for these practitioners as is partnerships with other authorities to allow safe and effective reporting that protects the victim.

Community-Driven Solutions

Communities have a significant role to play in tackling breast ironing. Given the deeply ingrained nature of harmful practices such as breast ironing, *Community-Driven Solutions (CDS)* are essential to change attitudes and behaviours that support these behaviours. We have discussed community-driven solutions more fully in our chapter on Investigation and Prosecution. Suffice to say, like other forms of harmful traditional practice, breast ironing requires solutions drawn from and working with affected communities. It is important to reiterate that CDS are not about accessing communities through gatekeepers, or paralegal processes, as these are very often driven or led by men and others discussing individual cases who may have a vested interest in maintaining the cultural practice. Instead the development of networks of influential community champions and role models from within affected communities are more effective options.

Challenges

Like other harmful traditional practices, a victim who has undergone breast 'ironing' is likely to come to the notice of authorities following a disclosure to a teacher, social worker, GP, midwifery service, breast cancer screening or other healthcare professional. As noted, it is important that the disclosure is managed carefully, with the aim of protecting the victim though multiagency

---

[12] HM Government, Working together to safeguard children, March 2015 accessed on 18 August 2017 via www.gov.uk/government/publications/working-together-to-safeguard-children%2D%2D2.

[13] Welsh Assembly Government, Safeguarding Children: Working Together Under the Children Act 2004, (2006) accessed on 18 August 2017 via www.gov.wales/topics/health/publications/socialcare/circular/nafwc1207/?lang=enf Section 47(1)(a)(ii) of the Children Act 1989.

partnerships. However, there are a number of significant challenges experienced when investigating cases of breast ironing and bringing perpetrators to justice. These include,

1. The majority of the offences take place when the victims and survivors are 8–12 years old. This presents significant problems in the gathering of evidence from the victim, who may not recollect the events (depending on when the police investigation is taking place) or may become confused about the sequence of the events potentially leading to conflicting or unreliable evidence;
2. This may be compounded if there is a need to access witness and professional evidence in foreign countries where there may be cultural support for the practice, or where evidence is obtained in other languages;
3. Investigators often have to establish, early on, whether the victim will support any prosecution, and this may be challenging because it is often close female relatives such as mothers, grandmothers and aunts that will be prosecuted;
4. The victim may require culturally sensitive support if they have been brought up to believe that this act was committed for their own good. This may also impact upon the victim's willingness to proceed with the prosecution;
5. There is likely to be a need to identify cultural and medical experts to support the investigation and prosecution. There are a number of academics and campaigners who can identify why it is practiced and distinguish between the cultural and regional variations in how the breast ironing is performed. There is however an absence of medical experts who can speak authoritatively on the longer-term impact of breast 'ironing'.

Summary and Recommendations

Breast ironing is very much a hidden form of abuse and there has to-date been limited research exploring its characteristics. This means that there is a dearth of knowledge about this harmful traditional practice. What little is known shows that it is a significant international problem, which disproportionately affects very young girls and causes substantial immediate and long-term negative health consequences. There is however no legislation currently in force in any jurisdiction specifically focussed upon breast ironing.

Given the damage that breast ironing causes to victims and survivors, and the expectations from various international agreements placed upon nation states to enshrine the rights of women into law, there is a strong argument for the development of specific legislation to outlaw this practice. In this regard, there is much that we can learn from how female genital mutilation (FGM) is managed across the justice system, the specific legislation and the development of relevant strategic partnerships. At the time of writing, in the UK there is considerable pressure upon government from civil society organisations to take action to introduce similar protections against breast ironing as for female genital mutilation (FGM). This includes the development of measures such as protection orders and mandatory reporting to increase the knowledge of the extent of this abuse, and to safeguard and protect girls being victimised or exposed to this practice.

7

Witchcraft, Spirit Possession and Belief-Based Abuse

This chapter explores harmful traditional practices motivated by a belief in witchcraft and/or possession by evil spirits. In most Western industrialised nations, witchcraft is generally considered to have been consigned to history. However, there is compelling evidence that abuse related to witchcraft and spirit possession is becoming increasingly prevalent.[1] This chapter reviews what is currently known about this type of abuse. It will identify the varied terminology used, the cultural and religious origins and the history of witchcraft legislation. Case studies will be used to highlight the characteristics of offending.

Definitions

One of the challenges in discussing this type of abuse is that at present there is no common language or nomenclature for this type of abuse.[2] The literature uses a myriad of different terms to label it. Terms such as, *ritual abuse, (ki)ndoki, ndoki, child sorcerers, the spirit world, the evil eye, djinns, black magic, voodoo, obeah, possession* and *witchcraft* are in common use. One difficulty is that these terms are often used interchangeably, and this leads to significant confusion. Indeed, many of these terms are vague, having numerous different

---

[1] Witchcraft-based child abuse: action plan launched, BBC News UK, 14/08.12 Available at: http://www.bbc.co.uk/news/education-19248144.

[2] Child Abuse linked to Accusations of 'Possession' and 'Witchcraft', Eleanor Stobart 2006 Department for Education and Skills.

© The Author(s) 2020
G. Campbell et al., *Harmful Traditional Practices*,
https://doi.org/10.1057/978-1-137-53312-8_7

meanings that can be specific to abuse in certain contexts, cultural groups or geographical locations. For example, the term 'spirit world' has different meanings across a range of religious and cultural contexts, some not necessarily associated with abuse; (ki)ndoki is a term specific to certain regions of Africa including Angola and the Democratic Republic of the Congo (DRC), and *ritual abuse* has most often been associated with satanic rituals, although can refer to any form of abuse that is associated with a ritual.

In an attempt to resolve some of these issues and to develop a common vocabulary, it is necessary to develop an operational definition of the practices we are referring to in this chapter. The terms most widely used by civil society, the public sector, faith-based and governmental organisations when discussing the forms of harmful traditional practice of interest here are *possession* and *witchcraft*. We will therefore use these terms throughout the chapter. Below we will attempt to provide a useful operational definition of these terms.

Christianity, Islam, Hinduism and indigenous religions are amongst the religions that support beliefs in possession by supernatural beings such as Gods, Satan and good or bad spirits. The term *possession* generally refers to a situation where it is believed that an evil force has entered an individual (most commonly, a child although older persons can be possessed) and is controlling them.[3] In the context of harmful traditional practices, the term *Witch* is most commonly applied to a child[4] (although is occasionally applied to an adult) who has an ability to use evil forces to harm others.[5,6] *Witchcraft* is therefore the behaviours and activities of a witch, usually involving the casting of spells or otherwise harming others.

As we discuss later, removal of an evil spirit is an important motivation for abuse and various terms have been used to describe this process. Three common terms have been identified[7]—*praying for children, deliverance* and *exorcism*. The most commonly used term for the removal of evil spirits is *exorcism*.[8] It appears that there are a range of behaviours associated with 'exorcism.' These range from 'praying for a child' while he or she is not present through

---

[3] 'Possession' can also be understood to include being taken over by a force for good, for example, the Holy Spirit.

[4] A child is considered to be a young person under the age of 18 years as defined by the Children Act 1989.

[5] Child Abuse linked to Accusations of 'Possession' and 'Witchcraft,' Eleanor Stobart 2006 Department for Education and Skills.

[6] For the practitioners of 'Wicca' and 'witchdoctors,' the term 'witch' can mean a person who is able to use good or evil forces for good or evil purposes.

[7] Child Abuse linked to Accusations of 'Possession' and 'Witchcraft,' Eleanor Stobart 2006 Department for Education and Skills.

[8] Stobart 2006, ibid.

to physical violence and torture towards the child designed to beat the evil spirit out of the child or to protect against the malign influence of witchcraft the child is held responsible for.

Exorcism has roots in Christianity and is frequently justified through Christian scriptural references,

Jesus gave his twelve disciples the power against unclean spirits, to cast them out, and to heal them all manner of sickness, and all manner of disease.[9]

In most cases, children are accused of witchcraft by either their families or church leaders or prophets, often from revivalist Pentecostal churches.[10]

Within the UK, there have been a number of child abuse cases where physical abuse was used as part of an attempted exorcism. Most notably the murders of five-year-old Victoria Climbie, five- or six-year-old 'Adam',[11] and

Case Study: Victoria Climbie

Victoria Climbie was born on 2 November 1991 in the Ivory Coast. In April 1999, at the age of 7 years she was brought to the UK by an aunt, Marie Therese Kouao, on the promise of a better education. It later emerged that Victoria had in fact been trafficked into France and the UK to assist her Aunt in maximising benefit claims such as housing allowances. In June 1999 a child minder had witnessed the aunt calling Victoria 'wicked' as well as noticing cuts to her fingers. By July 1999 her aunt had moved into a small bedsit with a new boyfriend, Carl Manning. Within eight months of them moving in together, on 25 February 2000, Victoria was dead, she was eight years old. She appears to have died as a result of hypothermia—indeed her temperature was so low it could not be recorded by hospital staff. In addition, she was malnourished and there were 128 injuries on her body. The injuries were a result of her being beaten with a bicycle chain, and a hammer had been used to hit her feet.

Victoria had been kept in inhuman conditions by her aunt. She was forced to sleep in a bath whilst being tied into a plastic bin liner with masking tape. She was often left like this for 24 hours or more.

Marie Therese Kouao and Carl Manning were tried and convicted of her murder at the Central Criminal Court (Old Bailey) in January 2001 and were each sentenced to a term of life imprisonment. Victoria experienced this level of physical abuse because Kouao and Manning believed that she was possessed by evil spirits and demons.

---

[9] Matthew 10:1.

[10] Cahn, 2006, pp. 422–423.

[11] In September 2001, the torso of 'Adam' was recovered from the River Thames. He has never been identified and no one till today has been held to account for his murder.

15-year-old Kristy Bamu.[12] To detail the sometimes severe abuse and neglect suffered by children in the context of faith-based abuse, we describe these cases in case-study boxes throughout this chapter.

Demographic Characteristics of Contemporary Beliefs in Witchcraft

Belief in witchcraft and spirit possession has been identified mostly, but not exclusively, in African countries such as Angola, the Central African Republic, Chad, the Democratic Republic of Congo, Gabon, Malawi, Nigeria, Swaziland and Tanzania as well as among associated diaspora communities. Such beliefs can and do influence broader policy making within countries where they are prevalent. For example, in 2013 the Civil Aviation Authority of Swaziland banned witches from flying higher than 150 metres on broomsticks,[13] stating that anyone doing so would be subject to arrest and a fine of R500,000 (about £35,000). The original purpose of the law was a legal response to the use of a drone by a private investigator, however the strong belief in witches in Swaziland meant that it was felt necessary to include witches in the legislation.

Other countries where child witchcraft allegations have been documented include Bolivia, Guatemala, Haiti, India, Indonesia, the Islamic Republic of Iran, Mexico, Nepal, Pakistan, Papua New Guinea, Thailand, Saudi Arabia and Syria.[14] Accusations of witchcraft and spirit possession linked to child abuse have also been recorded in Europe, in particular in the UK and France, mainly as a consequence of the migration of African and Bangladeshi communities.[15]

---

[12] In 2010, his sister and her boyfriend murdered 15-year-old Kristy Bamu on 25 October in Stratford. He was accused of being a witch.

[13] https://www.timeslive.co.za/news/africa/2013-05-13-broomstick-flying-witches-to-be-brought-down-in-swaziland/ accessed on 26 April 2020.

[14] Adinkrah, 2004, pp. 325–356; Bussien et al., 2011; Schnoebelen, 2009; B. Sleap, 2011; A. Cimpric, 2010; Bartle, Neville, 2005; P. Gibbs, 2010.

[15] Child Witchcraft allegations and human rights, European Parliament Directorate General for External Policies 2013.

Prevalence of Witchcraft, Spirit Possession and Belief-Based Offending

The true prevalence of this type of abuse is at present unknown. This is largely due to a lack of recording of these cases. For example, in 2015[16] figures obtained by the BBC under a Freedom of Information (FoI) request reveal that half of UK police forces do not routinely record these cases. Another FoI request to local councils across the UK in 2014 revealed 31 cases where a child had been accused of *witchcraft* or *possession by spirits*. In the last ten years the Metropolitan Police Service (MPS), London,[17] has reported a sharp increase in cases involving ritualistic and faith-based abuse having investigated over 83 cases. Young children seem to be most at risk; accusations of witchcraft and sorcery were most commonly directed at children aged between four and nine years of age.

As well as the lack of recording cases, reliable prevalence estimates are also compounded by limited knowledge of this type of abuse and a subsequent lack of identification among front line professionals.[18,19]

This form of abuse remains a hidden crime, therefore a better understanding of the belief systems operating within the affected communities must be developed in order to protect children and young people, who are at risk. Whilst the figures from the Metropolitan police reported above are likely an underestimation of the prevalence of this form of abuse, they do attest to the fact that it does exist within Western nations and abuse motivated in this manner is likely to be a significant cause of harm for children.

Beliefs About Witchcraft and Other Supernatural Entities

Witches throughout history were seen as capable of performing acts such as foretelling the future, creating thunderstorms and bad weather, turning day into night, causing the death of any enemy and moving unseen amongst the population. In order to cast their spells and perform rituals, body parts of the

---

[16] http://www.bbc.co.uk/news/uk-34475424 accessed on 17 September 2017.

[17] For further information, see Project Violet—The Metropolitan Police Service response to abuse related to faith and belief and www.met.police.uk/project violet video.

[18] BBC online 11 October 2015 'Witchcraft' abuse cases on the rise.

[19] Child witchcraft allegations and Human Rights Policy, Department DG External Policies.

innocent or uncorrupted (children and young babies) were thought to be used by the witch. These beliefs are not just confined to history, echoes of them can be seen in contemporary abuse. This is exemplified by the case of a young boy 'Adam', whose torso was found in the river Thames on 21 September 2001.

Case Study 'Adam': The Torso in the River Thames

The unsolved case of the 'Torso in the Thames' started as an unidentified body found floating under Tower Bridge on 21 September 2001. The boy was given the name 'Adam' by the Metropolitan Police Service as no family had claimed to have lost a child. This lent weight to the view that he had been unlawfully trafficked into the UK.

Following investigations, it was established that Adam's murder was a human sacrifice. It was likely that his fingers would have been removed as charms to give demonic strength, his blood would have been used to either bathe in or would have been drunk. His head would have been used as a cup or bowl or even drums. The colour of the shorts that had been placed on his body after death was likely significant to his killer(s), they were a red/orange colour which is the colour of resurrection or alternatively it may have related to the colour favoured by the deity to which the child was sacrificed.

The Scientific Picture of Adam

Adam's bones, intestines and skin were all analysed in the UK from which a clear forensic picture emerged of his country and place of origin, his movements in the last weeks of his life and his last meal. His bones were found to be rich in metal deposits found in specific regions of Africa—in particular the Yoruba plateau in Nigeria. The composition of his bones suggested that he had only spent about a month in Europe and the South East of England. This was confirmed by detailed analysis of the composition of his skin, which illustrated that his diet had changed dramatically in the four weeks prior to his death. Forensic examination of the contents of his large intestine found that his last meal had comprised mineral particles, clay pellets and rare plants including ground up bones and gold particles. These findings were consistent with his being recently trafficked to Europe and the murder being a human sacrifice.

The Nigerian police force confirmed that there are at least three murders a week in Nigeria as a result of human sacrifice to the Yarubin deities, of which there are 400. Sacrifices are often made to the god Shango, of thunder and lightning, a royal ancestor of the Yaruba, who particularly likes the colour red. Within this belief system, to kill a child is seen as an empowering act.[20]

There are a variety of other beliefs in supernatural entities relevant to understanding belief-based abuse. Many of which appear within the world's major religions. These include:

---

[20] Torso in the Thames Adams story 16 November 2011, Channel 4 documentary.

Djinns

The term Djinn or Jinn means literally 'hidden from sight/to cover/conceal' and is used to describe ghost/paranormal phenomenon throughout the Arabian countries and Central Asia. Djinns are usually considered to be invisible. A reference to Djinn is contained in the Holy Qur'an 15:27,

and the Djinn we created before from scorching fire.

The Prophet Muhammad is said to have noted three types of Djinn:

1. The type that has wings and they fly through the air.
2. The type that looks like snakes and dogs.
3. The type that stops and rests and then resumes its journey.

Djinns were also believed to sit in Solomon's Court,

And before Soloman were marshalled his hosts of Jinn, men and birds and they were kept in order of ranks.[21]

Djinns are believed to be both good and evil, assuming the shapes of humans, animals or wind. In modern times, self-styled 'healers' are consulted by communities who believe that a person may be possessed by a Djinn. The Djinn possession is considered responsible for ill-health, including mental illness. Healers are used as an alternative to qualified medical practitioners and may perform rituals, occasionally involving abusive acts, to summon and speak to the Djinn. This it is believed eases the effects of possession on the sufferer.

Voodoo

Voodoo is a religion of West African origin, practiced chiefly in Haiti and other Caribbean countries. It was born as a result of the transportation of millions of people as slaves from varying parts of Africa to Haiti and Cuba where aspects of Catholicism and the migrating beliefs intermingled to produce a religion that believes in the power of mother earth and the Virgin Mary.

---

[21] Qur'an 27:17.

Voodoo is a community-centred belief based on the visible world and the invisible world to which the dead transition. It combines elements of animism, magic and Roman Catholic ritual. It is characterised by belief in a supreme God, a large pantheon of local and tutelary deities, deified ancestors, and saints all of whom communicate with believers in dreams, trances and ritual possessions. The close link with nature also results in the worship of deities who dwell in rivers and valleys and who can be called upon to intervene and assist in daily life.

Voodoo has ordained clergy known as Hougan (priest) and Mambo (priestess), who offer guidance as requested, preserve rituals and maintain the relationship between the spirits and the community.

It is commonly believed that during meditation practices and rituals, spirits that are called upon will take possession of the body during a trance in order to express the spirits' wishes. Many ceremonies take place in cemeteries amongst the dead and it is regarded as a great honour to sleep on a close relative's grave. Death is regarded as the journey to meet ancestors. In Voodoo, followers believe that the spirits of the dead remain with the living as guardians and it is the calling up of the spirits in a ceremony that is often misinterpreted as being an evil act.

There is a darker side of Voodoo that involves the use of herbal powders, which range from harmless healing powders to 'zombie' powders that contain substances that induce a cataleptic state on inhalation.

JuJu

This is a spiritual belief system common to West Africa involving the use of amulets and spells during religious practice, to ensure compliance. Juju spells can be very powerful as agents of control of believers. For example, a Juju spell may be placed on women who are being trafficked in order to ensure that they remain mute and compliant as well as ensuring repayment of any alleged outstanding sums due to a trafficker.

The power of JuJu spells is aptly illustrated by a case in 2012. A sex trafficker was convicted on five counts of trafficking for sexual exploitation, rape and sexual activity with a child. He preyed on poverty-stricken orphans, tricking them into travelling to the UK with a promise of a better life. He performed a JuJu ceremony on his victims and survivors involving extracting samples of their blood and the cutting of their head and pubic hair prior to travel to the UK. The belief system is so powerful that even though the court case had concluded, the victims and survivors still strongly believed that they were tied to the contract they had made.[22]

Kindoki

Kindoki describes a belief in possession by evil spirits, specifically that a person can be possessed by evil spirits who have entered their body and need to be exorcised. It is also believed that unless the evil spirit is removed, it will inflict harm on others. Kindoki is also used to explain family misfortunes such as when families are experiencing stress due to economic or other factors including illness and disability. An accusation of Kinkodi may result from, the innocent, relaying of a dream by a child to a parent or carer, or should a person experience the onset of mental illness or dementia. It is estimated that over 50,000 of the children who are forced to live on the streets of Kinshasa have been left there by their parents because of a belief in Kindoki.

Another example of the effects of Kindoki can be seen in the Democratic Republic of the Congo (DRC). During the civil war, children made up the majority of combatants. It has been estimated that 30,000 child soldiers were to be found in the DRC. In the DRC, child soldiers were forced to commit various atrocities, acts which caused high levels of psychological trauma to the children. In explaining why, the children acted as they did, local churches have explained this as an example of Kindoki; in other words the children committed the acts because they were possessed by evil. This has meant that many of the children are unable to return to their homes for fear of persecution. Within the Kindoki belief system the way to 'cure' them and for them to be allowed back to their homes is by 'deliverance' or 'exorcism.' Exorcism has, as a result, become a huge business in the DRC.

The case of Kristy Bamu (see below) illustrates some of the features of Kinkodi.

---

[22] R V Osolase Canterbury Crown Court, 29 October 2012.

Case Study: Kristy Bamu

Kristy Bamu[23] and four of his siblings were visiting his sister Magalie Bamu and her partner Eric Bikubi in the UK when he was murdered. Magalie Bamu and Eric Bikubi were both from the Democratic Republic of the Congo and accused Kristy Bamu and his siblings of bringing 'Kindoki' into their home.

Bikubi told Kristy's sisters to jump out of a window to see if they could fly. They only escaped further violence by confessing that they were witches. Kristy refused to admit he was a sorcerer. He was therefore singled out for beatings as it was believed that he had cast spells on another child in the family.

Kristy was beaten with knives, sticks, metal bars and a hammer and chisel, as well as having floor tiles smashed over his head. By the time he was finally placed in a bath for ritual cleansing, he was 'begging to die'. He died on Christmas Day 2010, nine days after his arrival in the UK. There were 100 separate injuries to his body.

Kristy's sisters gave evidence that Magalie Bamu and Eric Bikubi were 'obsessed by witchcraft'. At the trial, Bikubi offered a plea to manslaughter on the basis of his mental condition; the plea was rejected by the Crown. On conviction for murder, Bikubi was sentenced to life imprisonment with a minimum term of 30 years and Bamu to a minimum term of 25 years. The trial judge stated the minimum terms reflected 'murder' with a 'sadistic element' including 'prolonged torture, mental and physical suffering prior to death'.

Muti

Muti is a term for traditional medicine in Southern Africa. The word Muti is derived from the Zulu word for tree, of which the root is -thi. In Muti, plants, animal bones and animal body parts are ground into a paste to release healing magical powers. In some cases, human body parts are used, as the use is believed to increase its powers.

It was thought that the case of 'Adam' described in the case study above was a Muti killing (although this was later rejected) due to similarities with other cases. These include, a 1960s unsolved discovery of a girl's torso in Epping forest, London, and the 1994 South African Police discovery of a body of an eight-year-old boy who had been the victim of a Muti killing. The remarkable similarities included that, in all the cases, the limbs had been amputated in a similar fashion and the bodies had been drained of blood.

---

[23] http://www.bbc.co.uk/news/uk-england-london-17255470 accessed on 17 September 2017.

History of Witchcraft Legislation

Witchcraft and possession have a long history in British law. it is interesting to explore this history as it aptly demonstrates how Western attitudes towards witchcraft have evolved, from strong belief in and a desire to protect the public from witches to a removal of all legislation predicted upon a broad rejection of their existence. It also serves to illustrate how these changing attitudes can be significantly at variance to those individuals who genuinely believe in witchcraft. This can lead many individuals from Western cultures, including many professionals, to be sceptical about the importance of witchcraft as a motivator for violent abuse, and may lead them to miss it.

Between 1542–1735 a series of Witchcraft Acts were passed by the English Parliament, which introduced serious penalties for the use of witchcraft. The first English statute criminalising the practice of witchcraft was introduced by Henry VII in 1542, followed by new, stricter, legislation by Elizabeth I in 1563 and James I in 1604.[24]

Witchcraft was punishable by death and forfeiture of the convicted person's chattels. It was forbidden to:

> *Use devise, practice or exercise, or cause to be devised or exercised, any invovacons or cojuracons of Sprites witchecraftes enchauntementes or sorceries to thentent to fynde money or treasure or to waste consume or destroy any persone in his body membres, or to pvoke (provoke) any persone to unlawfull love, or for any other unlawfull intent or purpose … or for dispute of Cryste, or for lucre of money digge up or pull downe any Crosse or Crosses or by such Invovacons or cojuracons of Sprites witchecraftes enchauntements or sorceries.*

By the Witchcraft Act of 1563, however, the death penalty was only imposed upon those who had caused harm and anyone who was able to read a passage from the Bible was spared from hanging. Although appearing to be merciful, more often than not those accused of witchcraft were at this time illiterate.

The Witchcraft Act, 1604, widened the range of offences where the death penalty could be applied to include those who invoked evil spirits or communed with familiar spirits. The Act imposed much harsher penalties for those convicted of witchcraft and also for anyone associating with or assisting them. The change in the attitude to the crime came from James I who himself

---

[24] Levack, *The Oxford Handbook of Witchcraft in Early Modern Europe and Colonial America*, p. 470.

had written on the subject in 1597 in *Daemonologie* where he warned against the practice of witchcraft. He supported his arguments with biblical and other texts. His personal attitude to witchcraft stemmed from a belief that he had been the intended victim of a murder plot by a group of witches in Berwick in 1590.

James I's reign saw one of the most notorious English witchcraft trials. On 18–19 August 1612, a number of men and women from the Pendle area of Lancashire stood trial for Witchcraft at the Lancaster Castle Assizes. Ten of these persons were executed by hanging the following day. This group became known as The Pendle Witches. The incident began when Alizon Device was begging. Having been refused money by a peddler, John Law, the peddler suffered a stroke. Although at first, he lost his speech, on regaining it, John Law told his son that Alizon had bewitched him. When she was brought to his bedside, she immediately confessed and begged for forgiveness. She was convicted by a jury on her own confession and was hanged with the others who stood trial similarly accused.[25] By 1683, the last witch to die in England pursuant to law had been executed.

In 1735, a further Witchcraft Act was introduced in the UK, which repealed the 1604 Act. This marked a complete reversal in attitudes. Penalties for the practice of witchcraft as traditionally constituted were replaced by penalties for the pretence of witchcraft. For example, a person who claimed to possess the ability to foretell the future was to be punished as a vagrant and a con artist, subject to fines and imprisonment.[26] The Witchcraft Act, 1735 remained in force until its repeal/replacement over 200 years later, by the Fraudulent Mediums Act 1951, which in turn was repealed as recently as 26 May 2008.

The last prosecution in England for a witchcraft-related death (although it was not the alleged witch that was executed but her killer) came in 1751 with the execution of John Colley in Hertfordshire who was hanged for leading a mob that attacked an old woman and murdered her by 'swimming' her in the local pond. This was a local test for a witch which involved tying the suspect's hand and foot, then throwing them into a pond or river. If they floated, they were deemed to be a witch and were taken out and hanged. The last person convicted under the Witchcraft Act 1735 was Jane Rebecca Yorke of Forest Gate in East London. In 1944, Yorke was convicted on seven counts of

---

[25] *1612 The Lancashire Witch Trials* by Christine Goodier 2011.
[26] Gibson, *Witchcraft and Society in England and America, 1550–1750*. A&C Black, p. 7.

'pretending … to cause the spirits of deceased persons to be present' and bound over to Keep the Peace.[27,28]

In the USA, witchcraft hysteria occurred with the Salem Witch Trials where between 1692–1693 over 200 people were imprisoned for witchcraft in Salem Village in Massachusetts.

Abusive Behaviour

Witchcraft, spirit possession and belief-based abuse frequently involves a mixture of the following,

1. **Physical abuse**: beating, burning, cutting, stabbing, semi-strangulating, tying up the child, or rubbing chilli peppers or other substances on the child's genitals or eyes.
2. **Emotional abuse**: in the form of isolation, for example, not allowing a child to eat or share a room with family members or threatening to abandon them. The child may also be persuaded that they are possessed.
3. **Neglect**: failure to ensure appropriate medical care, supervision, school attendance, good hygiene, nourishment, clothing or warmth.
4. **Sexual abuse**: within the family or community, children abused in this way may be particularly vulnerable to sexual exploitation.

As noted, abuse driven by a belief in witchcraft and spirit possession is often an attempt to remove an evil spirit by exorcism, or to protect oneself and others from an alleged witch. The practice of deliverance from an evil spirit often results in severe forms of abuse. These include, neglect by starvation in the belief that the evil spirit must be starved out, and physical violence in the belief that a child should be beaten to free the evil spirit.

'Deliverance' from the evil spirit can be instant, but more often is a gradual process and may involve the help of church pastors. It can involve prayer and also fasting or starvation of the child, coupled with physical abuse. Victoria Climbie (see case study) was beaten with bicycle chains and a hammer to her feet. A common factor in all the cases that have been tried in the courts is that the abuse has taken place within the homes of victims and survivors or abusers. Many of these characteristics of abuse can be seen in the case study of Child B, below.

---

[27] Chambers, The Witchcraft Act wasn't about women on brooms, 24/01/2007 (online). Available at http://www.theguardian.com/commentisfree/2007/jan/24/comment.comment3.

[28] *Living heritage: religion and belief* (online). Available at http://www.parliament.uk/about/living-heritage/transformingsociety/private-lives/religion/overview/witchcraft/.

Case Study: Child B

Child B was an eight-year-old orphan girl who arrived in the UK in 2002 from Cabinda, an Angolan enclave in the Congolese Territory, 200 miles from Kinshasa. She lived with her aunt. On 16 November 2003, she was branded as a witch at a church event. As a result of this, her aunt (who could not be named for legal reasons) and two others, Sita Kisanga and Sebastian Pinto, kicked, slapped and beat her until she admitted to practicing witchcraft. She was then cut with a knife on her chest, had chillies rubbed into her eyes and was starved in order to 'deliver' her.

She was found in the street on 24 November 2003 shivering, malnourished and drunk having been denied food and water for three days, been forced to drink alcohol, and had suffered 43 injuries to her body as part of the deliverance process. The three defendants were convicted of offences of child cruelty at the Central Criminal Court on 3 June 2005 and received sentences of ten years imprisonment. The trail judge said, 'It is the very pinnacle of cruelty to a child that demands the maximum sentence.'

Children from countries such as the UK may also be returned to Africa, in particular to the DRC, by their families for 'deliverance'. This is because these practices are widespread in the DRC and accepted as normal and necessary. For this reason, the 'deliverance' process may involve even more violent and extreme abuse. For example, a young boy sent by his mother from London to his grandparents in the DRC was made to fast on alternate weeks for two months. He had been told by his mother that he was travelling to Switzerland to be educated; he only realised on the plane that he was on his way to DRC. Until his mother had started attending a local church all had been well, but she was told that he had Kindoki and needed to be delivered. He suffered significant psychological and physical trauma as a result of his experiences.

Other forms of abusive 'deliverance' that have been documented include:

1. cutting a child with a razor blade to exorcise the evil spirit and sealing the wound with a special paste of chilli to prevent the spirit from re-entering the open wound;
2. stamping forcefully on the stomach of a child 'as the evil is locked deep in the stomach and the Kindoki needs to be drawn up';
3. 'cleansing the child's soul' by the washing saltwater into the eyes and drinking freshly killed pigeon blood, whilst the child kneels and recites 'get out in the name of Jesus';
4. forcing a child to drink hot palm oil.

Victim and Perpetrator Responses

It is important to note that the existence and identification of spirit possession, witches or witchcraft is a product of the belief systems of the accuser(s). Accusers genuinely believe that an individual is possessed or is a witch and they will often cite evidence such as spells that have been cast or the effect of alleged curses, in support of the claim. Where families hold these beliefs about a child, they are frequently terrified of the child and believe, with absolute conviction, that their safety, even their lives, is under threat from the child. As we have discussed, abuse often results because of an attempt to protect the family from the child and/or to drive out the evil spirit possessing the child. Abusers may genuinely believe that they are helping the victim, may feel justified in their actions, and may not consider their behaviour to be abusive or criminal.

As with other forms of abuse discussed in this book, individuals accused of being possessed or of being a witch may encourage and support the abuse. Some victims and survivors may not recognise their victimisation or may accept their fate believing that they deserve it as they are 'possessed' or are a witch. This is often because the victim may ascribe to the belief system and will state that they had been affected by an evil spirit, and as a result of deliverance are cured. This means that many victims and survivors may be unwilling to support investigations or prosecutions of their abusers.

Professional Responses

As we have described, like other forms of harmful traditional practice, this form of abuse can be complex involving unfamiliar (to Western eyes) belief systems, extreme forms of abuse and cross-border movement of victims and survivors and offending. As such no one agency or profession can hope to solve these issues alone. Like other forms of harmful traditional practices, abuse of this sort therefore requires a strong multiagency response to both prevent and investigate it, and to bring perpetrators to justice. In terms of a sustained approach to this form of abuse, there are a number of specialist groups that provide expert knowledge and investigatory expertise, and these can serve as model for the future.

Specialist Investigation Units: Project Violet

Due to the complex nature of this form of abuse involving widely held belief systems, the potential for cross-border offending and the challenges of cross-cultural policing, specialist units have been developed in some jurisdictions to help investigate and prevent this abuse. These units can be important as they act as sources of investigative and preventative expertise. They can also act as a hub where different agencies may connect and work together.

One example of a specialist unit exists within the Metropolitan Police Service, London. They have established a specialist team to investigate this form of offending codenamed Project Violet. This consists of a team of specialist officers with expertise and experience within this area who have established close working relationships with a variety of agencies and other professionals. These include government, border protection, social services and others. Interestingly, Project Violet has identified four main forms of child abuse linked to faith or belief that may be useful to other professionals in working with this form of abuse. These are:

- Abuse that occurs as a result of a child being accused of witchcraft or of being a witch (as seen in the Child B and Kristy Bamu cases).
- Abuse that occurs as a result of a child being accused of being 'possessed by spirits' that is, 'spirit possession' (as seen in the Victoria Climbie case).
- Ritualistic abuse (as seen the case of 'Adam').
- Satanic abuse.

Civil Society

Civil society organisations have an important place here as they can often provide cultural and belief-based expertise that can help other professionals to understand the abuse context. Because of their status as non-government organisations, they may also be better able to contact and engage victims and survivors. There are a few civil society organisations working in this area. The main organisation working to protect children subject to witchcraft accusations is Africans Unite against Child Abuse (AFRUCA), a registered charity in the UK centred on promoting the rights contained in the 1989 United Nations Convention on the Rights of the Child, in particular the rights and welfare of African children.

Summary and Recommendations

Witchcraft, spirit possession and belief-based abuse is complex in its characteristics, often involving extreme abuse committed for reasons that are difficult for many to comprehend. It is not however a 'thing of the past', the abuse is pernicious, causes terrible physical and psychological trauma, and if left unchallenged, victims and survivors continue to suffer sustained physical and psychological torture.

Local authorities, professionals and other public entities therefore have a duty to be more proactive in their approach. This will enable them to be better able to prevent further crime and abuse and to ensure that victims and survivors have access to the right specialist support. Given the damage that this form of abuse does to victims and survivors, it is also essential that longer-term support is provided for victims and survivors.

However, the levels of knowledge among various professionals concerning this form of abuse is low. This in turn means that recognition of victimisation is low, recording of crime is limited and so, whilst recognising that this form of abuse occurs, we have no knowledge of the true prevalence rates. Given this, public authorities, in particular police forces, health and social care professionals, need regular training in this form of abuse, its characteristics and consequences so that they can better recognise it, make timely interventions and ultimately protect and safeguard those exposed to it.

As with other forms of harmful practices discussed in this book, community-driven solutions are critical to challenging the superstition and myth, which drives such harmful belief systems. Professionals therefore need to be substantially more proactive in engaging with affected communities. Whilst arrests and prosecutions of perpetrators are essential in sending strong messages of support to victims and survivors and signalling to perpetrators that their offending will not be tolerated, the sustained support of the affected communities is fundamental to challenging mindsets and securing lasting change.

Finally, we recommend that it is important public authorities take a zero-tolerance approach to offenders. Individuals may argue that their behaviour is 'culturally', 'religiously' or 'traditionally' driven and may genuinely believe that they are 'protecting' the victims and survivors; however, being 'blind' to the effects of this abuse on the grounds that cross-cultural tolerance is an important feature of Western Society is not a viable option in our efforts to protect and safeguard children.

8

Other Harmful Traditional Practices

Here we present information about various other harmful traditional practices. For each of these, relatively little is known about them due to a dearth of research. Many of these practices are associated with the practices described earlier in the book, for example kidnapping can be associated with forced marriage, acid attacks are often involved in honour-based abuse. We present these other harmful practices here to acknowledge their existence, to provide professionals with more information about them should they encounter them, and in the hope that others may choose to research these practices in more detail in the future.

Acid Attacks

Acid attacks involve an attacker throwing or spraying acid in the face or body of the victim. This can lead to permanent disfigurement or scarring. It is more likely to be targeted at the face particularly in honour-based violence/abuse attacks predicated when a woman has allegedly brought shame on an individual or family, for example, suspected adultery or a woman has spurned an admirer's sexual attention or marriage proposal. A central motive is the idea that 'if I can't have you, no-one else can'. This method of attack is disproportionately targeted at women and girls by men. This is not a new phenomenon dating back to Victorian times in the UK and elsewhere.

A charity, Acid Survivors Trust International (ASTI) estimates that there are 1500 acid attacks recorded each year across the world, with 80% being

© The Author(s) 2020
G. Campbell et al., *Harmful Traditional Practices*,
https://doi.org/10.1057/978-1-137-53312-8_8

women. It is further estimated that 60% or 1 in every 6 such attacks go unreported.[1]

The Metropolitan Police Service data recorded only one acid attack over a 15-year period associated with an honour-related crime in 2011.[2] The authors assert that caution should be exercised in relation to this data due to widespread under-reporting of honour-based violence/abuse.

In the UK corrosive materials are also used in domestic abuse, robberies and assault attacks by individuals and criminal gangs. Irrespective of the corrosive product used, such attacks are often referred to as acid attacks.

Bride Kidnapping/Bride Abduction

This is where a girl is kidnapped or abducted by an individual, or a group (the latter being most common in this type of offending) who wish to force the girl into a marriage that she and her family would not otherwise consent to. This also happens when a girl has shunned a male's advances.

In honour cultures however, if a girl is kidnapped and held in the company of her male kidnapper(s), even where this is clearly against her will, her virtue is irredeemably compromised. Indeed, in honour cultures, the kidnappers may be supported by female relatives. Data provided by the NGO Women Support Center,[3] suggests that there are at least 11,800 cases of forced abduction of women and girls every year in Kyrgyzstan. Of these victims and survivors more than 2000 reported being raped too.[4] Some estimates say that 50% of all marriages in Kyrgyzstan are from bride kidnapping.[5]

Bride Price

This is the price paid by a groom or his family to a girl's family in exchange for the girl in marriage. The price can be land, property, cash, cattle, cash, food or a combination of these items. The price is also linked to the status and purity

[1] http://www.asti.org.uk/a-worldwide-problem.html accessed on 17 November 2017.
[2] http://www.bbc.co.uk/bbcthree/item/5d38c003-c54a-4513-a369-f9eae0d52f91 accessed on 17 November 2017.
[3] Women Support Center http://www.wsc.kg/ accessed on 17 November 2017.
[4] http://www.unwomen.org/en/news/stories/2013/2/new-law-in-kyrgyzstan-toughens-penalties-for-bride-kidnapping accessed on 17 November 2017.
[5] https://www.huffingtonpost.com/entry/kyrgyzstan-bride-kidnapping_us_57d05dede4b03d2d4597eef5 accessed on 17 November 2017.

of the girl. In some cultures, it is seen as a sign of man's intention to look after his bride and is an accepted practice. Indeed, in some cases the exchange of property is described as being symbolic.[6] However, this practice further demonstrates the low status of women in some cultures where they are traded as property and is linked to Child Early Forced Marriage. This practice is different from dowry (see below).

Criminalisation of Adultery

The criminalisation of adultery in some cultures often results in a woman being subjected to corporal punishment. This is because adultery is often deemed to have been the woman's fault for entering into the relationship, and that she tempted the man into the sexual relationship. It is also important to note that, in some honour cultures, if a woman has been in the sole company of a male who is not a relative, this is enough to allege adultery which will be punished.

Dowry Violence and Abuse

Dowry is the amount of property or money brought by a bride to her husband on their marriage. They can include the transfer of land, property, money or other valuables. Dowries have a long history in Europe, South Asia, Africa and other parts of the world. Historically, dowries were provided when a bride went to live with her husband's family and was intended to ensure she was looked after, and the bride and her children would have assets if she was ever to be widowed. Dowries would be arranged or negotiated before the wedding. The size of the dowry is associated with a bride's family wealth and status. Importantly, dowry can be used to build the power, strength and status of the man's family.

In some communities, dowries continue to be expected, and demanded as a condition to accept a marriage proposal. This can have a significant financial impact on the bride's family. India outlawed the system of dowry in 1961 in the form of The Dowry Prohibition Act 1961; however, the practice still

---

[6] http://www.bbc.co.uk/news/world-africa-33810273 accessed on 17.

continues with crime associated with it going un-reported for fear of reprisals and other severe repercussions.[7]

Disputes related to dowry, often related to securing an increase in the dowry, sometimes result in acts of violence and abuse against women and other family members. The severest of cases can result in honour killings, arson attacks and serious physical assaults caused by acid attacks and the like. Such violence and abuse can take place before or after marriage.

It is of note that many charities or civil society organisations[8] across the UK are recording serious crimes and abuses associated with dowry. However, UK police forces are not recording dowry violence and neither is it mentioned in HM Government, Police or CPS Strategies.[9]

Early Pregnancy[10]

This refers to pregnancies in children. Early pregnancy can have significant harmful consequences for both young mothers and their babies. Babies of teenage mothers tend to be born premature, have low birth weight and are more likely to die in the first year of life.

The mortality rate for young mothers is high with some dying in labour through heavy blood loss and other complications. Poor health through the lack of nutrition causes further complications.

Fattening Ceremony Before Marriage[11]

Fattening ceremonies or forced feeding before marriage is common among the Akwa-Ibom, Efik, Anaang and Ibibio people found in Akwa-Ibom and Cross River states of Nigeria, Mauritania (here it is referred to as Leblouh) and Cameroon.[12] It is intrinsically linked to Child Early Forced Marriage.

---

[7] https://pulitzercenter.org/projects/asia-india-dowry-marriage-violence-against-women-bride-culture-husband-physical-mental-sexual-suicide accessed on 17 November 2017.

[8] Charities including The SHARAN Project, Iranian & Kurdish Women's Rights Organisation, Sahil Project and Karma Nirvana have recorded cases of dowry violence.

[9] http://www.independent.co.uk/news/uk/crime/shunned-beaten-burnt-raped-the-dowry-violence-that-shames-britain-9803009.html accessed on 17 November 2017.

[10] http://www.ohchr.org/Documents/Publications/FactSheet23en.pdf accessed on 17 November 2017.

[11] Ibid.

[12] https://www.theguardian.com/world/2009/mar/01/mauritania-force-feeding-marriage accessed on 17 November 2017.

Before marriage, the bride, often a young girl, is locked up in a room and over-fed for her new husband. In some cultures, this is geared towards making the girl more sexually appealing to her husband, as slimmer women are considered unfit for marriage.

The significant health risks associated with this practice include obesity and associated risk of heart diseases, stroke, diabetes and risk of difficult delivery of children due to macrosomia. Foetal macrosomia is caused by genetic factors and maternal factors, for example, obesity or diabetes.

Female Infanticide and Son Preference[13]

Some communities prefer sons to daughters. This is most apparent in countries where the prevalence of the male line to preserve land and property is paramount. Sex bias or son preference places the female child at a significant disadvantage from birth. In such cultures the female child is seen as a burden on families. In some communities, particularly in Asia, the practice of son preference drives female infanticide with the termination of a female foetus through medical or more crude procedures.

Scarification[14]

This involves deliberate cutting of a body part as a treatment for diseases like swollen abdomen, low back pain, chest pain, fractures, dislocations, eye problems and so on.

For example, in Nigeria's Edo state the Esan people use scarification to treat a child with malaria or sickle cell anemia with crude and unhygienic cutting around the area of the spleen on the abdomen, often without anaesthesia. In Kenya both boys and girls of the Massai may have circular scars branded onto their cheeks under their eyes, in a practice designed to prevent eye problems. They also may have their front teeth removed in a practice designed to prevent lock jaw. The Wukaria people of Taraba State, Nigeria remove the epiglottis in boys and girls to make breathing easier. This leaves the child exposed to choking and respiratory tract infections. There is no medical evidence to support any of these practices.

---

[13] http://www.ohchr.org/Documents/Publications/FactSheet23en.pdf accessed on 17 November 2017.
[14] http://www.nimedhealth.com.ng/harmful-traditional-practices-updated/ accessed on 17 November 2017.

Tribal body scaring, body piercing including lip plates, are used in Uganda, Sudan, and Ethiopia to decorate the body of men and women. They are used as signs of tribal, clan, cultural identity and belonging, and as part of an initiation ceremony into adulthood, to define rank and status, show of strength and as a sign of beauty. These markings define social, economic and political status.[15]

All of the above practices have significant health risks. Crude methods and crude implements are used in many of the above procedures, often without anaesthesia or any form of infection control. This results in pain and significantly raises the risk of infections such as HIV, hepatitis B, tetanus, and heavy blood loss. In addition, psychological trauma can also result.

Sexual Violence and Forced Pregnancy

In conflict zones, sexual violence and forced pregnancy through rape is employed as a harmful tactic against the civilian population to abuse and control them. It is also used to suppress ethnic or religious communities.

The 1998 Rome Statute[16] and United Nation's Security Council Resolution 1325[17] in October 2000, both recognised that sexual violence in conflict is a form of gender-based violence, is a war crime, a crime against humanity and an act of genocide.[18] In June 2014 the UK's then Foreign Secretary William Hague and Angelina Jolie, Special Envoy for the UN High Commissioner for Refugees, co-chaired the Global Summit to End Sexual Violence in Conflict in London.[19] Of note over 120 countries were represented at this event, which was also attended by in excess of 1000 experts, faith leaders, youth organisations and national and international civil-society organisations. The Global Summit committed to breaking and ending the taboo surrounding wartime rape, end its use and 'shatter the culture of impunity', with which the perpetrators act. This was reinforced with the launch of an International Protocol

---

[15] https://afrolegends.com/2015/09/16/scarification-an-ancient-african-tattoo-culture/ accessed on 17 November 2017.

[16] https://www.icc-cpi.int/nr/rdonlyres/ea9aeff7-5752-4f84-be94-0a655eb30e16/0/rome_statute_english.pdf accessed on 17 November 2017.

[17] UN, Security Council, Resolution 1325 (2000) S/RES/1325 (2000) accessed on 17 November 2017 via https://documents-dds-ny.un.org/doc/UNDOC/GEN/N00/720/18/PDF/N0072018.pdf?OpenElement.

[18] http://www.un.org/womenwatch/osagi/wps/ accessed on 17 November 2017.

[19] https://www.gov.uk/government/topical-events/sexual-violence-in-conflict accessed on 17 November 2017.

on the Documentation and Investigation of Sexual Violence in Conflict,[20] which includes setting out international standards on how to collect information and evidence and protecting witnesses.[21]

Stoning or Flogging

This is a form of capital punishment, which affects women and can affect men. Often the victim is buried up to the neck, with rocks then thrown at them. This results in a slow and painful death.

Flogging is a non-lethal form of punishment. However, it does result in serious injuries. It is practiced as a form of punishment in a number of countries including Afghanistan, Indonesia, Iran, Nigeria, Pakistan, Sudan and Saudi Arabia.

Both of these practices are used for punishment as part of honour-based abuse or other harmful practices with often disproportionate impact on women, for example, the criminalisation of adultery.

Vani, Wani or Swara

Vani, Wani or Swara is a harmful practice found in parts of Pakistan and Afghanistan whereby a young girl is forcibly married as part of a punishment for a crime committed by her male relatives. It is a form of Child Early Forced Marriage. It can be decided by a tribal council of elders or assemblies—referred to as a jirga, panchayat, panchayat raj.[22] It is also frequently linked to blood feuds or other disputes.

---

[20] Foreign & Commonwealth Office, International Protocol on the Documentation and Investigation of Sexual Violence in Conflict, *Best Practice on the Documentation of Sexual Violence as a Crime or Violation of International Law* (March 2017) accessed on 17 November 2017 via https://www.gov.uk/government/uploads/system/uploads/attachment_data/file/598335/International_Protocol_2017_2nd_Edition.pdf.

[21] Foreign & Commonwealth Office, Chair's Summary – Global Summit to End Sexual Violence in Conflict (June 2014) accessed on 17 November 2017 via https://www.gov.uk/government/publications/chairs-summary-global-summit-to-end-sexual-violence-in-conflict/chairs-summary-global-summit-to-end-sexual-violence-in-conflict.

[22] https://tribune.com.pk/story/264445/child-marriage-12-year-old-girl-given-in-wani-to-85-year-old/ accessed on 17 November 2017.

Virginity Tests[23]

The practice of virginity testing take place in wide range of community, cultures, religious groups and countries throughout the world. Here the virginity of a bride is considered an important virtue. Virginity testing is essentially used to determine a girl or young woman's purity. However, there is no accurate or reliable test for a girl's virginity and it rests upon the perceptions (often subject to their own biases) of those doing the testing. This is a key driver for some forms of FGM. It is also important to note that there is no similar test for boys or young men.

Widow Burning, 'Sati' and Stove Burning

In patriarchal societies a woman derives her social status from that of her husband. In the absence of a husband, a woman does not have any status and is regarded solely as property. Some widows are sexually and physically exploited, deemed outcasts and suffer social isolation.[24] Sati is an attempt to avoid this situation by self-immolation.

A related practice is stove-burning. This practice originally involved a woman being burned by the deliberate tampering with a stove causing an explosion. Another version of this occurs where a woman is soaked in a stove's fuel, such as kerosene oil, before being set on fire. This is often associated with honour-based abuse, widows, or other forms of cultural punishment for perceived wrongs.

Wife Inheritance and Maltreatment of Widows[25]

Some property and inheritance laws can be grossly unfair to women, often leaving them and their children in situations of great dependency or in a state of destitution. Within some cultures it is expected that a widow will marry or enter into a sexual relationship with the brother, or other kinsman of her late husband. This practice occurs in a number of countries including Kenya, Malawi, South Africa, Zimbabwe, India and Siberia. In affected communities

---

[23] http://www.thedebrief.co.uk/news/real-life/virginity-testing-around-the-world-20160160621 accessed on 17 November 2017.

[24] UN, Widowhood—invisible women, secluded or excluded. Published by Published by the Division for the Advancement of Women/DESA (December 2001).

[25] http://www.stopvaw.org/harmful_practices_types_prevalence accessed on 17 November 2017.

there is a belief that the widow *owes* her in-laws a child or children in return for maintaining her property rights in any inheritance she may receive. In practicing countries, widows are also exposed to other forms of harmful practices, violence and abuse including sexual violence, forced marriage and trafficking.

Refusal by a widow can lead to her being 'disinherited', ostracised from the family and/or community, and thrown out of her home, which is likely to be then seized by the late husband's family. In some cultures, there are extreme versions of the practice where the widow is forced or coerced to have sexual intercourse with a social outcast in order to cleanse her husband's evil spirits.

Summary and Recommendations

In this chapter we have highlighted a range of abusive behaviour that can be classified as forms of harmful traditional practices. In general, legislation does not exist that explicitly refers to these practices; however, the abusive and criminal nature of them is often covered within other legislation that can be applied. As we have noted there has been little research done into these practices and we therefore have relatively limited knowledge about them. For the future we recommend that research is conducted to explore the nature, motivation, prevalence, victim and perpetrator characteristics of these practices. We also recommend that existing legislation is explored to ensure that there are effective means of prosecuting these practices where necessary.

9

Police Investigation of Harmful Traditional Practices

In this chapter, we discuss effective approaches to investigation of harmful traditional practices by the police. Police investigation is a critical stage of the criminal justice process, and investigative failures can have terrible consequences. These include the continuation of abuse through to the death of victims. Here we consider legal frameworks governing investigations and the challenges harmful traditional practices present investigators.

Police Service's Roles and Responsibilities

To begin, it is perhaps pertinent to consider the roles and responsibilities of the police. In England and Wales, the mission of policing is enshrined in the Police Service Statement of Mission and Values. Despite priorities changing, over time this has remained consistent. The overriding mission is:

> to make communities safer by upholding the law fairly and firmly; preventing crime and antisocial behaviour; keeping the peace; protecting and reassuring communities; investigating crime and bringing offenders to justice.[1]

This accords with three core policing principle:

---

[1] NPCC, APCC accessed via https://www.npcc.police.uk/documents/Policing%20Vision.pdf on 28 April.

1. Protection of life and property
2. Prevention and detection of crime
3. Maintenance of HM The Queen's Peace

The policing mission is underpinned in the UK by the Human Rights Act 1998, the Equalities Act 2010 and the Code of Ethics.[2] The police service must take all necessary steps to ensure that the fundamental human rights of those who have contact with them are protected. This obligation extends to victims and survivors of gender-based violence and harmful traditional practices.

To support the achievement of the police mission and to maintain consistency of approach throughout the country the United Kingdom's College of Policing has issued Authorised Professional Practice (APP) guidelines. These are compiled in consultation with police subject matter experts, professionals in relevant government departments, academics and civil society organisations. APP has been developed in relation to FGM, forced marriage and honour-based abuse[3] although not so far for other harmful practices discussed within this book. There is APP guidance for other areas not specifically about but relevant to the policing of harmful traditional practices. These include, investigation, critical incident management, missing persons, rape and sexual offences, modern slavery, risk assessment and management, prosecution and case management.

Police forces and their Crown Prosecution Service (CPS) counterparts have also developed an investigation and prosecution protocol designed to help obtain best evidence in cases of the harmful traditional practices, FGM, honour-based abuse and forced marriage.[4] Whilst no similar guidance is yet available for breast ironing, witchcraft and other forms of harmful cultural practice, the aforementioned protocols can provide some guidance for police officers investigating them.

---

[2] College of Policing, Code of Ethics (July 2014) https://www.college.police.uk/What-we-do/Ethics/Documents/Code_of_Ethics.pdf accessed on 28 April 2020.

[3] https://www.app.college.police.uk/app-content/major-investigation-and-public-protection/forced-marriage-and-honour-based-violence/.

[4] http://www.cps.gov.uk/publications/agencies.hbv_and_fm_protocol_nov_16.pdf *and* http://www.cps.gov.uk/london/assets/uploads/files/fgm_protocol_cps_mps_2013.pdf accessed on 26 August 2017.

Principles of Investigation

As in other jurisdictions, a cornerstone of British Policing is policing by the consent of the public and this is underpinned by the extent to which the public has confidence in the police.[5] To build and maintain public confidence, the police have a responsibility to ensure that investigations are carried out professionally, ethically and to an agreed high standard. The College of Policing Investigation APP therefore highlights the following principles, applicable to all investigations including those of harmful traditional practices[6]:

1. the exercise of legal powers should not be oppressive and should be proportionate to the crime under investigation
2. as far as is operationally practical and having regard to an individual's right to confidentiality, investigations should be carried out as transparently as possible victims and survivors , witnesses and suspects should be kept up to date with developments in the case
3. investigators should take all reasonable steps to understand the particular needs of individuals, including, but not limited to, any protected characteristics they may have, in order to comply with the provisions of the Equality Act 2010
4. investigators should have particular regard for vulnerable people and children and investigators should respect the professional ethics of others. This is particularly important when working with those whose role it is to support suspects.

Cultural Awareness

As we have seen in previous chapters, harmful traditional practices are nested within culturally defined traditions. As such an awareness of the cultural context of the alleged offence is central to effective investigation. *Cultural awareness* allows investigators to develop insight to better understand victims and survivors, witnesses and perpetrators. This can be gleaned from an

---

[5] https://www.gov.uk/government/publications/policing-by-consent/definition-of-policing-by-consent accessed on 25 August 2017.
[6] https://www.app.college.police.uk/app-content/investigations/introduction/   accessed   on   25 August 2017.

examination of the characteristics of the offending type (as discussed in the various chapters within this book) and of affected families and communities.

However, it is essential to draw a distinction between cultural awareness and cultural sensitivity. *Cultural sensitivity* is the process through which the police and other professionals should, rightly, be sensitive to the cultural context within which they operate and to avoid, where possible, giving offence to communities through insensitive comments and activities. However, there are limits to cultural sensitivity for investigators. Over sensitivity can give rise to indecision and inaction. However, where cultural traditions serve to support offending and abuses, as in the case of the practices discussed in this book, they should rightly be challenged and cultural sensitivity should not be a reason not to act. Indeed, in cases such as those discussed here, too greater focus upon cultural sensitivity may serve to maintain abuse if it leads to inaction. The Chief Her Majesty's Inspector of Constabulary (HMIC) Inspector, Sir Thomas Winsor made this point forcefully,

> *Cultural traditions and sensitivities deserve and should always be given due respect. But where they operate to imprison vulnerable people behind barriers of fear and the threat or reality of violence, and facilitate or intensify crimes committed against them, such barriers must be broken. They deserve no respect at all....*[7]

Care therefore needs to be taken by investigators to be culturally aware and behave in respectful ways towards a community's members whilst at the same time being alive to and being prepared to act decisively against allegations of abuse even if it is claimed by members of the community that the alleged abusive acts are acceptable cultural traditions or religiously mandated.

Proactive engagement work with the communities and others is crucial if the police service is to deliver its services in an effective and efficient way. This includes actively working with communities affected by harmful traditional practices, the wider community, statutory agencies (including social care, health, education, local authorities, children and adult safeguarding boards etc.) and specialist NGOs. Roberts et al. (2013) have considered in detail effective approaches for police when engaging with communities in order to prevent HBA and other harmful traditional practices.[8]

---

[7] HMIC, The depths of dishonour: Hidden voices and shameful crimes: An inspection of the police response to honour-based violence, forced marriage and female genital mutilation (December 2015).

[8] Roberts, K. A., Campbell, G. and Lloyd, G., 2013. *Honor-based Violence: Policing and Prevention* (CRC Press).

Depending on the effectiveness of the delivery of its services, it is however possible for the police to easily lose the support and confidence amongst communities.[9] An example of this relates to prosecutions for FGM: following the first prosecution for FGM in the UK, campaigners warmly welcomed and were supportive of the police response; however , a dearth of subsequent prosecutions has led to diminishing confidence in police and their approach to FGM.[10]

The Skills of an Effective Investigator

It is important for investigators to remember that any investigation is an attempt to collect relevant facts and versions of events and that it should be conducted in a non-discriminatory and proportionate way. In order to achieve this, the UK College of Policing's APP for Investigation identifies a range of knowledge and skills that investigators need[11]:

- effective planning and creative thinking;
- effective decision making;
- evidential evaluation, that is, determining the investigative and evidential value of material and information gathered during the investigation;
- confidence to challenge expert opinion;
- victim and witness care, that is, ensuring that the needs of victims and survivors and witnesses are central to investigative action;
- use of investigative methods that do not affect victim, community or partner confidence in the police service or negatively affect the outcome of the investigation;
- integrity, common sense and sound judgment;
- respect for people's human rights;
- treating people with dignity and respect.

---

[9] https://www.publications.parliament.uk/pa/cm201617/cmselect/cmhaff/390/39006.htm#_idTextAnchor028 accessed on 25 August 2017.

[10] http://irokoheritage.co.uk/fgmuk-welcome-relief-after-first-fgm-prosecutions-announced/ accessed on 16 November 2017.

[11] https://www.app.college.police.uk/app-content/investigations/introduction/ accessed on 25 August 2017.

Investigation Priorities

The ultimate goal of any investigation, if proven that a crime(s) has taken place, is to resolve it to the satisfaction of the victim(s). The priorities for any police investigation, however, are the same regardless of the offence investigated. Core investigation priorities should include:

- Preservation of life (protection of life and safeguarding).
- Preservation of a crime scene(s) to maximise the recovery of evidence.
- Securing other evidence.
- Identifying victims and survivors and witnesses.
- Identifying suspects.[12]

Key Considerations in Investigating Harmful Traditional Practices

Investigations of harmful traditional practices are frequently complex, often involving conspiracies between family members and others and can result in serious offences such as homicide. There are many risks in these investigations, where a lack of knowledge can lead to indecision and a lack of action that may prove fatal. It is important therefore that all staff, particularly those with public-facing roles, to receive appropriate training in recognising the warning signs of various harmful traditional practices and effective ways of responding to them.

The risks involved in investigating harmful traditional practices are clearly illustrated by the murder of Banaz Mahmod described in the case study below. This case highlights failings at all stages of the investigation, from first reports to police through to inadequate case management and risk assessment. As the case study highlights, at many stages there were opportunities to take steps that may have prevented the murder.

---

[12] In harmful traditional practice cases it should be remembered that it is likely more than one suspect will be involved and these cases may involve a conspiratorial network of offenders within the family, extended family and/or the community.

Case Study: The Murder of Banaz Mahmod, 2006

Banaz Mahmod was born in Iraqi Kurdistan on 16 December 1985. Aged 10 years Banaz moved to the UK with her family where they claimed asylum. When she was 17 years old Banaz entered into an arranged marriage with a man 10 years her senior. Two years later following sexual and physical abuse Banaz left him and returned to live with her parents in Mitcham, Surrey (London Borough of Merton). Following this separation, Banaz formed a new relationship with another man, which was deemed by her male family members as being 'unsuitable'.

As this relationship was considered unsuitable, Banaz and her boyfriend were followed and surveilled by community members, and they were seen to kiss outside a London underground station.

In December 2005 Banaz's paternal uncle Ari Mahmod called a family meeting, where she was deemed to have brought shame upon her family by her actions.

Between September 2005 and January 2006, Banaz came into contact with police officers from the Metropolitan Police Service and West Midlands Police on five occasions, during which serious allegations including sexual assault and threats to kill were made. The Independent Police Complaints Commission (IPCC) would later find there were deficiencies in how some police officers responded to and investigated these allegations,[13] which also amounted to misconduct.

Incident 1—On 14 September 2005: Banaz went to Croydon Police Station to make allegations about physical and sexual assault. The offences took place in Coventry, so the matter was transferred to West Midlands Police, who have jurisdiction of this area. No meaningful investigative steps were taken by the Metropolitan Police investigators or a supervising manager.

The IPCC investigation identified that allegations against three MPS officers were partially substantiated, including a Detective Inspector failing to correctly manage the sexual assault investigation, a trainee Detective Constable failing to take the necessary steps to locate/arrest the suspect or carry out intelligence checks and a Constable failing to speak to Banaz in person to carry out a full assessment of her allegations.

Allegations against three West Midlands police officers were also substantiated including a Detective Constable, who conducted a flawed investigation as it was not carried out in a timely and appropriate manner, a Detective Sergeant, who failed to adequately supervise the investigation and a Detective Inspector, who was aware of the lack of progress in the investigation, but who failed to take pro-active action.

Incident 2—On 4 December 2005, Banaz attended Mitcham Police Station where she reported that on 2 December, her mother had received a telephone call from Ari Mahmod, in which it was alleged that Ari had threatened to kill

(continued)

---

[13] IPCC, Independent Investigation – Executive Summary, Contact between Banaz Mahmod and the Metropolitan Police Service and West Midlands Police September 2005–January 2006 (November 2008).

(continued)

Banaz because she had been seen kissing her new boyfriend and had brought shame on the family.

Incident 3—On 10 December 2005, a police officer attended Banaz's family address in response to a complaint of threatening phone calls. Banaz told the officer that she had received a silent phone call on the house phone on 6 December and received a further call from a Kurdish man on 10 December.

Incident 4—On 31 December 2005 a neighbour of Banaz's grandmother alerted police that the glass panels of her side door had been broken. Banaz had broken the glass in a desperate bid to escape from her father as he plied her with brandy. Banaz ran into a nearby café and staff and customers saw that she was distressed and that her hands were bleeding. Banaz told them she had been forced to drink alcohol; that people were 'after her' and that she had to break a window to escape. The Ambulance Service and Police were then dispatched to the scene. Banaz told the ambulance crew that she had broken a window and that her father had forced her to drink alcohol and was trying to kill her. She also said that 'they' were going to kill her boyfriend (Mr Rahmat Suleimani).

The Control and Dispatch system was updated with the following comments

Female; self-harmer; smashed window and bleeding from arms.

The two attending police officers questioned Banaz about the broken window. They were apparently told by witnesses (although not Banaz herself) that she had claimed someone was trying to kill her. One of the police officers noted that Banaz was *'drunk'*, *'very dramatic'* and *'kicking and screaming'*. The officer warned Banaz that she needed to *'calm down'* or she would be *'arrested for criminal damage'*.

Banaz was taken to hospital and the police officers visited the damaged property's owner. The owner did not pursue an allegation. The officers then attended Banaz's home and spoke to her parents. Her father claimed he had dropped Banaz off at her grandmother's house to do some cleaning.

Had the officers conducted an effective primary investigation e.g. adequately debriefing and interviewing witnesses, they may have identified the threat that Banaz's father posed to her and to her boyfriend.

In comments to police, her boyfriend, Rahmat, stated that Banaz told the police officers that she believed her father and uncle wanted to kill her. In addition, the nursing staff also stated that they had been told by Ms. Mahmood that her life was under threat and that she was in fear of her father and uncle. The lead police officer advised a police inspector of her intention to *deal solely with the criminal damage matter* (as Banaz hadn't told her directly about the threat to life offence)—although ambulance staff, members of the public and nursing staff knew of this threat.

The same lead investigator visited Banaz at the family home on 4 January 2006 in order to finalise the damage (to the window) matter. Asked if everything was fine Banaz could only nod a 'yes'.

Incident 5—During the evening of 22 January 2006, Banaz's boyfriend was approached by four men, whom he knew. They asked him to go with them and when he refused a threat was made to his and Banaz's life. He attended Kennington Police Station the following day to report the matter. However, the

(continued)

(continued)

police station reception officer *didn't record the matter*. That same day—23 January, Banaz attended Mitcham Police Station to report the threat. She told a police officer the names of the men who had threatened her boyfriend, although she was not a witness to the incident. Banaz disappeared soon after this.

On 25 January 2006, Banaz was reported missing by Rahmat. The Metropolitan Police Service (London) began a three-month, high-risk missing person inquiry. On 29 April 2006 Banaz's decomposed body was found in a suitcase buried in a shallow grave in a rear garden in Handsworth, Birmingham.

On 11 June 2007, Banaz's father, Mahmood Mahmood, her paternal uncle, Ari Mahmood, and another relative, Mohammed Hama, were convicted of her murder and sentenced to life imprisonment. (Other Iraqi Kurdistani community members stand convicted of crimes associated with Banaz's murder, for example, perjury and preventing the lawful and decent burial of Banaz).

Suicide of Rahmat Suleimani

Another tragic outcome of this case was that in March 2016 Rahmat Suleimani, who had been in police protection over previous last 10 years, died in hospital after apparently taking his own life. He had made two previous suicide attempts. Rahmat was quoted as saying, '*My life depended on her. She was my present, my future, my hope. She was the best thing that had ever happened to me. My life went away when Banaz died. There is no life. The only thing which was keeping me going was the moment to see justice being done for Banaz*'. Rahmat was another victim of Banaz's honour killing. Rahmat is another honour-killing victim.

The so-called honour killing of Banaz Mahmod acted as a catalyst for changes to how the police forces in England and Wales investigated and responded to honour-based violence and abuse cases. The case also dramatically influenced police forces knowledge and understanding of HBV/A.

Primary and Secondary Investigation

Police investigations can be divided into two broad components, *primary investigation* and *secondary investigation*. Primary investigation refers to all of the activities that should be undertaken following a *first report* of an offence, these include actions such as obtaining initial details about the offence and making initial responses to protect a victim. Secondary investigation refers to the next phases of an investigation *after the initial actions* and includes actions such as interviewing witnesses, identifying and arresting suspects. Below we explore some of the key considerations in investigating harmful traditional practices that may minimise some of the risks and help investigators to conduct effective investigations. (A detailed account of the investigation of honour-based violence and abuse can be found in Roberts et al., 2013).[14]

---

[14] Roberts, K. A., Campbell, G. and Lloyd, G., 2013. *Honor-based Violence: Policing and Prevention* (CRC Press).

Primary Investigation

First Reports to the Police

As with other crime types, harmful traditional practices come to the notice of the police in variety of ways. These may include:

- A victim or witness may directly approach police via phone, attendance at a police station, a community event or other direct contact.
- A support agency may approach the police directly to report their suspicions of victimisation.
- Police may receive a referral from an NGO, or independent third party such as a teacher, social worker or health care worker.
- An indirect report to police. That is, a report to the police service for matters other than harmful traditional practices either from the victim, a witness or third party. This may include family members who are responsible for abuse. Other matters frequently reported include, domestic abuse, child abuse, missing persons, theft allegation against a family member, crime by the victim, victim suicide attempt or self-harm, absenteeism from school, crime in action—kidnapping, false imprisonment, threats to kill.
- An approach from an employer or co-workers.[15]

Victims and survivors show a great deal of courage in reporting their experiences. Their reports often follow repeated threats, assaults and intimidation, that may have continued for years. In addition, in making the report the victim faces an increased risk of further assaults, abuse and victimisation often because they will be perceived to have violated community norms.[16] Hence all organisations and professionals should work on the basis of the *One Chance Rule* (highlighted in the UK Government's Forced Marriage Multi-Agency Practice Guidelines) in their engagement with victims and survivors and witnesses. That is to say, given the high risks of future severe abuse to victims/survivors and witnesses, there is a need to respond quickly and effectively to reduce this risk and prevent offending. Professionals should therefore assume

---

[15] Harmful traditional practices in the workplace. http://clok.uclan.ac.uk/32803/7/32803%20Harmful%20Traditional%20Practices%20in%20the%20Workplace%20-%20Guidance%20for%20Best%20Practice%202020.pdf.

[16] University of Bristol, Victim/survivor voices – a participatory research project Report for Her Majesty's Inspectorate of Constabulary Honour-based violence inspection (August 2015, pages 16, 17).

that there is just 'one chance' to act, and should respond immediately to all reports of harmful traditional practices.[17]

Attitude and Approach of Primary Investigators

The attitude and approach of the primary (and secondary) investigating officer is vital in securing the victim's confidence and trust in the police and their ongoing cooperation both with the investigation and advice from police. Indeed, investigations are much more effective in obtaining useful evidence and information where victims and survivors have confidence that they are being listened to, are believed and are being taken seriously. This in turn engenders trust in police and maximises victim and witness cooperation with the police. Trust in police can be seriously compromised if not lost all together where the approach, demeanour and attitude of the investigator signals cynicism or disbelief and this can have tragic consequences.[18] For example, in the case of Banaz Mahmod, an attitude of disbelief seems to have pervaded the police response and this led to inaction. To engender trust, the investigator must therefore be supportive of the victim. They must listen carefully to their account of events and take their concerns seriously. Investigators should also make clear that they are there to help and take appropriate action to protect victims and survivors. Essentially, victims, survivors and witnesses have got a fundamental right to be listened to and heard.[19]

Victim Safety

In any investigation, the safety of the victim must be the overriding concern for police first responders and police investigators. Keeping victims and survivors safe is also fundamental to victims having confidence in the police and the investigation.[20] In order to do this, as well as furthering the investigation, the primary investigator needs to identify the victim's context and the threats and risks faced. This means being aware of the cultural context and the

---

[17] https://www.gov.uk/government/publications/handling-cases-of-forced-marriage-multi-agency-practice-guidelines-english accessed on 25 August 2017.

[18] Roberts, K., 2010. Great expectations: Relations of trust and confidence in police interviews with witnesses of crime. *Policing: A Journal of Policy and Practice*, 4(3), pp. 265–272.

[19] National Police Chiefs' Council (NPCC), Honour-Based Abuse, Forced Marriage and Female Genital Mutilation: A Policing Strategy for England, Wales & Northern Ireland 2015–2018 (December 2015).

[20] Ibid.

associated warning signs of harmful traditional practices. For example, *why is the 'A' star student suddenly doing things that they wouldn't normally do, such as shoplifting, harming herself or regularly absenting herself from school?* It is essential for the primary investigator to affect an investigative mindset, asking pertinent questions and exploring issues as they arise without prejudging the situation. The investigator must try to answer several core questions:

- *Why is this happening now?*
- *What are the risks to the victim and where do they come from?*
- *Why does the victim need to be protected?*
- *What is the suspect's motivation(s) and their capabilities?*
- *What do I need to do now to protect the victim and others?*

Risk Assessment and Risk Management

Importantly, the primary investigator must identify risks faced by the victim and act accordingly. Risk assessment is a process involving the identification, assessment and prioritising of the threats of harm (actual and perceived) to an individual(s). Risk management is the process by which resources are coordinated that are aimed at mitigating, the identified risks. It is important to note that the perception of risk and harm by a victim must not be underestimated as victims and survivors are often the best judges of the risks that they face. The victim's fears should NOT therefore be overtly dismissed by investigators.

The risks identified in a risk assessment should be prioritised in terms of the threat of harm, the nature of that harm, where and when the harm may occur. These then need to be incorporated into a risk management plan that is sensitive to these contingencies. For example, some threats are likely to cause greater harms than others and may be more imminent than others. So, should it be clear that a victim faces an imminent risk of harm, immediate steps to protect them should be taken. This may include taking them into protective custody or other similar action.

In England and Wales, the only accredited model for primary frontline[21] and secondary investigators to use, assess, identify and manage risk is the Domestic Abuse, Stalking, Harassment and Honour Based Abuse (DASH)

---

[21] Sometimes referred to as first responders.

2009 model.[22] This tool is useful as it provides a structured method for investigators to consider risk. The quality and effectiveness of this tool is however only as good as the assessor, the extent to which they are alive to relevant factors, their level of effective engagement with victims and survivors, their specific knowledge of harmful traditional practices, and their possession of as much relevant information as possible. Invariably, the risks faced by victims and survivors of harmful traditional practices and the witnesses who support them are significant, including threats to kill, murder, rape, seriously assault, kidnap, false imprisonment, intimidation and harassment, and damage to their property. The authors argue that it is important that police officers and other public authority officials who are likely to come into contact with victims/survivors and witnesses of harmful traditional practices should be trained in risk assessment, identification and management. A common risk model must also be used for all working in this field to achieve a common understanding and common response to managing the risks faced by the victim.

Data Storage

The safe handling, management and storage of the victim's personal data are also integral to the victim's perception of personal safety. Given the ethnic and cultural diversity of the modern police service and other public authorities, there is a possibility that some officers may be from cultures and communities affected by harmful traditional practices and supportive of them. Because of this, the potential accessibility of a victim's personal data is a core concern. It is therefore essential that public authorities have appropriate restriction levels to victim and witness personal data. This may entail controlling access to data through access restrictions to crime/incidents reports, intelligence reports (local force intelligence systems and national, e.g. Police National Database), missing person reports, and inter-force case transfers. Authorities need also operate regular audits to ensure that there has been no unauthorised access and/or disclosure of data. It is also important that there are appropriate policies in place for supervisors and colleagues to safely manage, protect and secure the well-being of employees who identify themselves as a victim or potential victim of such crime types.

---

[22] http://www.college.police.uk/News/College-news/Documents/Risk-led_policing_of_domestic_abuse_and_the_DASH_risk_model.pdf accessed on 3 September 2017.

Other Tasks for First Responders

First responders are also required to take the following actions in accordance with the UK National Police Chief's Policy:

1. Take the victim's photograph, fingerprints and a DNA sample with her/his informed consent. This supports a police investigation should a victim go missing and the police mount a missing person investigation. The samples allow the investigators and other officials to identify the victim.
2. Complete a family tree with the support of the victim. This allows investigators to have a complete understanding of the structure of a victim's family in the UK and overseas (as appropriate).
3. Place the victim's personal details onto the Police National Computer (PNC). This allows the police and other law enforcement officers to have an awareness of the victimisation and to provide an alert if the victim is found in another location or in circumstances of concern. Any locate trace marker of the victim/survivor's personal details placed onto the PNC should be the subject of periodic review by the police service in accordance with any operating human rights legislation. This is particularly important for those victim/survivors over 18 years old.

Primary Investigation Dos and Don'ts

For an effective primary investigation of harmful traditional practices there are a number of do's and don'ts. These summaries, the information above and some additional considerations are detailed in Table 9.1 below.

Secondary Investigation

As stated, harmful traditional practices are complex offences and can involve multiple perpetrators and high risks of harm for the victims and survivors. Accordingly, they can be difficult to investigate. We therefore recommend that any police secondary investigation should be conducted by *specialist investigators*. Specialist investigators should be trained detective officers with enhanced training in harmful traditional practices, especially honour-based abuse. In addition, it is the authors' experience that better investigative outcomes and improved service delivery to victims/survivors and witnesses occurs when specialist investigators operate within bespoke specialist units such as,

Table 9.1 Dos and Don'ts for primary investigators in investigations of harmful traditional practices

DOs	DON'Ts
Manage the case professionally, sensitively and with confidentiality.	Do not approach the victim's family.
Speak and interact with the victim and witnesses with understanding and empathy.	Be judgmental and interact with the victim/survivor or witnesses in a matter-of-fact way.
Take action to maximise the recovery of evidence including identifying and protecting victims/witness/perpetrators/crime scenes.	Do not take action which compromises people's safety and evidence.
Conduct an immediate review of the risk assessment and management issues affecting the victim and other people, e.g. children.	Do not recommend the victim to undertake mediation.
Develop a risk management or safety plan, which includes an escape plan and safe methods of contact.	
Do handle, store and transfer the victim's personal details with care and confidentiality	Do not reveal details of the case to anyone outside the investigation or the 'circle of trust'. The circle of trust would include IDVA (Independent Domestic Violence Advisor), Specialist caseworker—NOT a local councilor, mayor, MP or other people in public life and/or positions of authority.
Do manage the case on a 'need to know' basis.	Do not make subjective judgements about the victim her/his lifestyle, culture or religion.
Reassure and support the victim whilst ensuring that timely and regular updates are provided using the victim's preferred method of contact.	Never use a family member (particularly a child), community member, friend or any other unauthorised person to interpret.
Be honest, open and transparent with the victim.	If there is an international dimension to the case never make direct contact with foreign law enforcement agencies or government officials.
Ensure that a manager is briefed to provide advice, guidance and resource support, e.g. Tactical Advisor.	Don't ever state that this is NOT a job for the police service.
Refer the victim to a culturally specific trusted civil society organisation.	

(*continued*)

Table 9.1 (continued)

DOs	DONTs
Only use authorised and approved interpreters.	Do not use children, other family members or witnesses as an interpreter.
Ensure that an accurate record of documented decisions is maintained.	
Refer to a specialist investigation unit, e.g. Community Safety Unit, Public Protection Unit.	

in the UK, Community Safety Teams and Safeguarding Teams. Such specialist units bring together multi-agency expertise to provide 'one stop' investigative and victim support. We would therefore recommend such an approach to the investigation and management of harmful traditional practices.

As with any criminal investigation, the secondary investigator must review the actions of the primary investigator to ensure that every opportunity has been taken to secure evidence, identify/arrest the perpetrator(s) and that the risks to the victim and any other person affected, for example, witnesses is/are being effectively managed.

Every effort must be made to conduct the investigation to the satisfaction of the victim and to secure an outcome, which meets the victim's needs and expectations. For some victims and survivors , this may not mean seeking a criminal justice outcome (see the later chapter on alternative dispute resolution).

Victim and Witness Interviews and Statements

As in any investigation it is of critical importance to secure the victim and any significant witness evidence as soon as practicable using the medium of Achieving Best Evidence (ABE) video interviews. Importantly, these can be used as evidence in chief during criminal trials. We will turn to the subject of interview shortly in this chapter.[23]

The continuous communication and safe engagement with the victim and witnesses is very important to gain, maintain confidence and trust in the police investigation and any ensuing court proceedings. In addition, risk assessment and management strategies for victim safety must be continuously

---

[23] https://www.cps.gov.uk/publications/docs/best_evidence_in_criminal_proceedings.pdf accessed on 25 August 2017.

reviewed as changing circumstances entail changing risk of harm. The secondary investigation should also consider consulting subject matter experts, for example, an individual who has an enhanced theoretical and practical understanding of harmful traditional practices in the context of the relevant cultural dynamics, to enhance their contextual understanding and to develop other potential lines of inquiry. Cultural experts may also be able to provide help in developing interview strategies for witnesses and victims and survivors and to explain aspects of evidence to the investigator.

Interviewing Victims and Survivors

The authors believe that victims and survivors must in all cases be treated as *significant witnesses* as set out in the UK Ministry of Justice Guidance.[24] This guidance defines a significant witness as those who:

- have or claim to have witnessed, visually or otherwise, an indictable offence, part of such an offence or events closely connected with it (including any incriminating comments made by the suspected offender either before or after the offence); and/or
- have a particular relationship to the victim or have a central position in an investigation into an indictable offence.

In addition, a victim's other family members and any partners of victims and survivors should also be deemed to be significant until their status within the investigation can be fully determined.

There are two main ways to present the evidence of a victim or witness, that is, Criminal Justice Act (CJA) 1967, s 9 *(written) statement,* or through a *video interview.* We believe that due to the circumstances associated with harmful cultural practices, victims and survivors are also very likely to fall into the category of *intimidated witness.*[25] In law, *intimidated witnesses* are defined as those witnesses whose evidence is likely to be diminished by reason of fear or distress.

Given this and as noted above, it is the authors' recommendation that evidence should be obtained from all victims and survivors of harmful traditional practices by way of a video interview conducted in accordance with the principles of *Achieving Best Evidence* and the *Youth Justice and Criminal*

---

[24] https://www.cps.gov.uk/publications/docs/best_evidence_in_criminal_proceedings.pdf accessed on 25 August 2017.

[25] Special measures are set out in the Youth Justice and Criminal Evidence Act 1999.

Evidence (YJCE) Act 1999 Section 17 of that act for intimidated witnesses. The lead investigator must notify the Crown Prosecution Service of the desire to make an application for these special measures as soon as possible after the perpetrator(s) is/are charged/prosecuted in order for it to be considered and presented to the court for a judicial adjudication to be made.

One major advantages of video interviews is that, under the Youth Justice and Criminal Evidence Act 1999, the video product may be used as primary evidence in criminal proceedings.[26] A major benefit of this is that recorded evidence can serve to limit any negative effects of the criminal justice system upon victims and survivors, that is, their account is able to be given without them having to face the perpetrator(s) who may intimidate them in a court setting. This also means that the victim's voice will be heard in court proceedings should the victim go missing, is untraceable, or has been murdered. The importance of this is illustrated by the case studies, below, describing the rape and kidnap of Ceri Linden and the murder of Tulay Goren.

Case Studies: Ceri Linden[27] and Tulay Goren

Ceri Linden

Thirty-four-year-old Masood Mansouri was convicted of the rape and kidnap of 20-year-old Ceri Linden following an incident in August 2014. In the days following the crimes the victim's account was recorded on video by police investigators. Sadly, the victim took her own life soon after. The victim's video interview was used as evidence in chief at Mansouri's trial following which he was convicted. Mansouri appealed against his conviction; however, the Appeal Court Judges judged that his conviction was 'safe'.

The Honour Killing Tulay Goren

Tulay Goren was murdered by her father in 1999 because she was in an unapproved relationship with an older man. Tulay was alleged to have breached the honour code. Her body has never been found. In 2004, the Metropolitan Police Service reopened the investigation into Tulay's murder. Tulay's mother, Hanim, provided evidence at court that she saw Tulay lying tied up and bound on a bedroom floor, as did Tulay's sister Hatice. Hatice tragically died in a road traffic crash in 2006.[28] However, her evidence was heard in court in the form of a video recording of her Achieving Best Evidence (ABE) interview she gave to the police investigators. Following an 11-week trial at the Central Criminal court (otherwise known as the Old Bailey), Tulay's father was convicted of murdering his daughter after she was kidnapped, drugged and bound. He was handed down a life sentence with a minimum that he serves a minimum of 22 years of imprisonment. Tulay's body has never been recovered.

---

[26] Youth Justice and Criminal Evidence Act 1999, Section 27.

[27] http://news.bbc.co.uk/1/hi/england/london/8332811.stm, Honour case girl 'kissed goodbye' BBC News, 29 October 2009.

[28] http://www.telegraph.co.uk/news/uknews/crime/6832862/Honour-killing-father-convicted-of-murder-of-Tulay-Goren.html accessed on 9 September 2017.

Victim and Family Liaison

It is essential during an investigation that the victim is provided with reassurance and an honest and regular briefing as to how the investigation is progressing. A lack of updates by the investigator only serves to undermine the victim's confidence in the investigation. Depending on the seriousness of the crime or incident under investigation, the authors recommend that either an accredited family liaison officer (FLO) or another officer is assigned to liaise directly with the victim.

For homicide cases in the UK, a FLO will always be appointed to liaise with a victim's family to offer support, advice and guidance whilst updating them on the progress of the police investigation. FLOs are also investigating officers and so will act under the direction of the Senior Investigating Officer (SIO) to gather evidence and intelligence as they go about their duties.

A 'suspect in the family' homicide (as is the case with many honour killings) is a difficult deployment for a FLO as she/he is likely to meet the suspect(s), who may try and debrief them on the evidence being gathered during the investigation. Indeed, even after a suspect(s) has been arrested and prosecuted, family members, who remain loyal to the suspect(s), may attempt to find out and communicate investigative developments to the suspect(s). This is often done so that family members can be seen to be protecting the family's honour, in the eyes of both the suspect(s) and the wider community.

There are various considerations that should be made before deploying a FLO, some of which are identified by the College of Policing APP for Investigation, these include[29]:

- A FLO strategy must have been developed (and this should be regularly reviewed as the investigation develops). The strategy should include:

  - Setting out parameters of contact with the family and managing their expectations.

- FLOs must be fully briefed before deployment so that they understand the parameters of their deployment.
- The presence of suspect(s) within the family and risks presented to the FLO.
- Risk management must be considered before deployment.
- Occupational health and other support for the FLOs. FLOs who are not appropriately supported can very quickly become stressed and 'burnt out'.

---

[29] https://www.app.college.police.uk/app-content/investigations/victims-and-witnesses/#family-liaison-strategy accessed on 25 August 2017.

- FLO should be deployed in pairs
- In complex cases a Family Liaison Advisor should be appointed
- Where multiple FLOs are deployed a Family Liaison Coordinator should be appointed
- the FLO should be selected on the basis of their capability, capacity, skills, knowledge and experience. This includes consideration of their:

  – Cultural and/or religious knowledge.
  – Language skill.
  – Have good communication and inter-personal skills.
  – Be compassionate and be able to empathise.
  – Appropriate gender. Here the gender of the victim and their comfort working with members of the other gender should be considered.
  – Psychological impact on the officer(s) deployed.
  – Honour-based abuse knowledge of the FLO.
  – FLOs should always be

  a qualified investigator.
  occupationally qualified as FLOs.

The Use of Interpreters

The police have a legal duty under the[30] Police and Criminal Evidence (PACE) Act 1984 Code C, to make sure that appropriate arrangements are in place for the provision of a suitably qualified interpreter at the police station, for a detainee who is deaf or whose first language is not English. In addition, it is also incumbent on defence solicitors to ensure that the interpretation needs of their clients are met.[31]

The growing diversity of the UK means that the use of interpreters is an important consideration. Given the deeply ingrained cultural and collective nature of harmful traditional practices it is essential that the most appropriate interpreter is found. An appropriate interpreter can in contrast be trusted not to disclose evidence outside of the investigation, will not make subjective judgments about the victim, does not practice or condone harmful cultural practices, and does not otherwise prejudice the investigation and prosecution.

[30] Police and Criminal Evidence Act 1984 Codes of Practice C, D and H.
[31] Law Society, Use of Interpreters in Criminal Cases Practice Note (October 2015).

In contrast, a corrupt interpreter may seek to elicit favour from community members by exposing what the victim has told the police investigators, damaging the investigation and endangering the victim.

Whilst interpreters must always highlight declarations of interest, it is also incumbent on the police investigator and prosecutor to exercise due diligence in understanding the credentials of the interpreter they intend to commission. In the exercise of due diligence, it is important that interpreters should be chosen from the National Register of Public Service Interpreters (NRPSI) and the Signature Directory.[32] There are also a number of key considerations in identifying an appropriate interpreter:

- That the interpreter is competent and qualified to interpret and translate into the language that they state they are qualified to operate in.
- The gender of the interpreter, particularly if the victim is a female and is being asked about intimate details of crimes committed against her.
- The culture and religion of the interpreter relative to the victim.
- Where the interpreter and their family come from (both in the UK and overseas if relevant). It needs to be established if there is any potential for a community connection to the perpetrator.

Secondary Investigation Dos and Don'ts

Similar to the primary investigators there are a number of 'dos and don'ts' for the secondary investigator in the investigation of harmful traditional practices (see Table 9.2).

Joint Working Between the Police and the Crown Prosecution Service

Cases of harmful traditional practices require teamwork between the investigator and the prosecutor. The CPS Legal Guidance—*CPS and Relations with the Police*—states that the police may seek CPS advice at any stage of an investigation. Early investigative advice may well save police and CPS resources later and assist in the management of the risks associated with such offending.[33] This advice should also lead to police obtaining higher quality evidence,

---

[32] Formerly the Council for the Advancement of Communications with Deaf People.
[33] http://www.cps.gov.uk/legal/a_to_c/cps_relations_with_the_police/ accessed on 26 August 2017.

Table 9.2 Dos and Don'ts for secondary investigators

DOs	DONTs
Review all of the actions and decisions of the primary investigating officer/ first responder.	Reinforce any ill-informed decisions and/ or actions of the first responder.
Manage the case professionally, sensitively and with confidentiality.	Approach the victim's family or seek to get involved in any form of mediation.
Speak and interact with the victim and witnesses with understanding and empathy.	Be judgmental and interact with the victim and or witnesses in a matter-of-fact way.
Take action to maximise the recovery of evidence including identifying and protecting victims/witness/perpetrators/ crime scenes.	Take action which compromises people's safety and evidence.
Regularly review the risk assessment and management issues affecting the victim and other people, e.g. children, people who have been supporting the victim. Develop and review the risk management or safety plan, which includes an escape plan and safe methods of contact.	Reveal details of the case to anyone outside the investigation, or the 'circle of trust'. The circle of trust would include the IDVA (Independent Domestic Violence Advisor), Specialist caseworker—NOT a local councilor, mayor, MP or other people in public life and/or positions of authority.
Handle, store and transfer the victim's personal details with care and confidentiality.	Make subjective judgements about the victim her/his lifestyle, culture or religion.
Manage the case on a 'need-to-know' basis.	Never use a family member (particularly a child), community member, friend or any other unauthorised person to interpret.
Reassure and support the victim whilst ensuring that timely and regular updates are provided, using the victim's preferred method of contact.	If there is an international dimension to the case never make direct contact with foreign law enforcement agencies, or government officials.
Be honest, open and transparent with the victim.	Don't ever state that this is NOT a job for the police service.
Ensure that a manager is briefed to provide advice, guidance and resource support, e.g. Tactical Advisor, Family Liaison Coordinator, Family Liaison Officer, Interview Advisor, Forensic Manager.	
Review the actions of the first responder, e.g. have fingerprints, DNA and a photograph with the victim's informed consent and a family tree developed.	
Refer the victim to a culturally specific trusted civil society organisation.	

(continued)

Table 9.2 (continued)

DOs	DON'Ts
Refer the case to a specialist prosecutor in line with the joint NPCC and CPS protocols. (http://www.cps.gov.uk/publications/agencies/HBV_and_FM_Protocol.pdf accessed on 26 August 2017).	
Only use authorised and approved interpreters.	Use children, other family members or witnesses as an interpreter.
Ensure that an accurate record of decisions is maintained.	Directly contact law enforcement, or government official in another country.
In HBA/FM cases, do contact the UK Government's Forced Marriage Unit if your case has an international element to it.	
Consider using cultural and other experts to advise during the investigation. Know exactly why you are engaging an expert. Always exercise due diligence in checking the credentials of the experts and language interpreters being employed.	

which should in turn lead to an increase in successful prosecutions. In particular, the CPS Director's Guidance on Charging (5th Edition) notes that[34]:

Prosecutors may provide guidance and advice in serious, sensitive or complex cases and any case, where a police supervisor considers it would be of assistance in helping to determine the evidence that will be required to support a prosecution or to decide if a case can proceed to court.

The CPS and the police are working together to improve investigation and prosecution performance including the development of a joint police / CPS stakeholder group, updates to CPS guidance, quality assurance process to review the flagging of forced marriage cases, and joint conferences to identify good practice and lessons learned.

---

[34] https://www.cps.gov.uk/publications/directors_guidance/dpp_guidance_5.html accessed on 26 August 2017.

Summary and Recommendations

In this chapter, we have described how investigations are guided by the police service's core policing principles and have identified the key processes involved in the conduct of an effective investigation. We have discussed the relationship between the effectiveness, the quality of a police investigation and public confidence in and cooperation with the police. We have also shown how it is also vital for a victim/survivor to have confidence and trust in the police to maximise their cooperation with investigations.

Victims/survivors and witnesses face a tremendous pressure in reporting their own families and communities to the police. This presents significant risks to them and anyone supporting them. They will face ostracism from their families and communities as this is often seen as a betrayal of family, community and cultural identity.[35] In addition, victims and survivors frequently do not wish to criminalise parents, siblings, other family members, or have their cultural group or religion demonised in the media. Investigators need to be cognisant of these issues and how they may affect the all concerned and the overall investigation.

As previously highlighted, the CPS and the police are committed to working together to improve the investigation and prosecution of harmful traditional practices. In order to improve performance, there have been updates to the CPS's guidance as well as the implementation of a quality assurance process to review the flagging of forced marriage cases proving an added layer of scrutiny and support. In addition, a joint police / CPS stakeholder national group has been formed, which is complemented by joint conferences to identify good practice and lessons learned.[36]

There are also significant challenges following the conclusion of the police investigation and any court cases; criminal and/or civil. Sadly, some victims and survivors, weakened by the isolation and fear of retaliation, succumb to their family's false promises of reconciliation and offer of a safe haven. The reality is, of course, very different for those victims and survivors who return. They are often forced to lead a life of subjugation, servitude and abuse. Investigators also need to be aware of this risk and consider engaging civil society organisations to support the victim following the conclusion of the

---

[35] University of Bristol, Victim/survivor voices – a participatory research project Report for Her Majesty's Inspectorate of Constabulary Honour-based violence inspection (August 2015).

[36] CPS, Violence Against Women and Girls Report 2018–19, pp. 19 and 20 https://www.cps.gov.uk/sites/default/files/documents/publications/cps-vawg-report-2019.pdf.

investigation or court case. This may well prevent further offending following what appears to be a conclusion to a case.

The principles discussed in this chapter, if applied to investigations, should maximise the collection of high-quality evidence, minimise the risks to victims and survivors and prevent future offending.

10

Prosecuting Cases of Harmful Traditional Practices

Following from the previous chapter concerned with police investigations, this chapter explores important considerations for the prosecution of cases of abuse related to harmful traditional practices. We will explore effective principles for police and prosecutors working together, the use of expert and non-expert witnesses and the admissibility of their evidence in prosecutions, the role of civil society organisations such as the UK Forced Marriage Unit, court procedures and the management of victims and survivors, use of special measures, and current challenges for police and prosecutors. The aim of this chapter is not to provide a definitive account of all the issues relevant to prosecuting these cases, but to highlight some important issues that prosecutors will need to consider.

Police and Prosecutors Working Together

Cases of harmful traditional practices require teamwork between the investigator and the prosecutor. It is essential that the investigator and the prosecutor approach such investigations as a partnership team to better serve the victim and witness needs. This helps to ensure the right support is provided to victims, survivors and witnesses, the evidence obtained is understood and evidential gaps are identified. Given this, the Police Service and the CPS have developed joint Investigation and Prosecution Protocols for honour-based

© The Author(s) 2020
G. Campbell et al., *Harmful Traditional Practices*,
https://doi.org/10.1057/978-1-137-53312-8_10

violence/abuse, forced marriage and female genital mutilation, although not for other forms of harmful traditional practice.[1]

At the start of a criminal investigation these protocols should be activated. Police officers and prosecutors must comply with this guidance to ensure that charging and other prosecution decisions are fair and consistent, and fully comply with PACE, the PACE Codes of Practice and the Code for Crown Prosecutors.

In general, specific cases involving a death, rape or other serious sexual offence should always be referred to a local Area Prosecutor as early as possible and, in any case, once a suspect has been identified and it appears that continuing investigation will provide evidence upon which a charging decision may be made. Wherever practicable, this should take place within 24 hours in cases where the suspect is detained in police custody (this is the period of relevant time permitted by the Police and Criminal Evidence Act 1984 for the majority of crimes) or within seven days when they have been released on bail or released under investigation.[2] Where a case is referred to the CPS at an early stage, the prosecutor may determine what information needs to be provided by the police, the stage at which the evidence will be reviewed, and the test of this evidence that will be applied.

Prosecutors, as per the Director of Public Prosecution's Guidance, should make charging decisions in all cases that have not been allocated to the police, as per the Director of Public Prosecution's Guidance.[3] In making decisions the CPS prosecutor should refer to the CPS Legal Guidance for prosecutors relating to FGM, Honour Based Violence/Abuse and Forced Marriage as appropriate.[4] These legal guidance documents detail the key points that prosecutors need to consider when reviewing cases.

A recent HMIC and HMCPSI Joint Inspection Report[5] has however highlighted areas for improvement in the joint working relationship with the police service. It recommended that the UK College of Policing, in conjunction with the CPS, produces a set of national learning that as a minimum, include the operation of the Director of CPS Guidance on Charging[6], the

---

[1] http://www.cps.gov.uk/publications/agencies/HBV_and_FM_Protocol.pdf accessed on 26 August 2017.

[2] Section 37(2) Police and Criminal Evidence Act 1984. The Policing and Crime Act 2017 introduced 'release under investigation' as an alternative to pre-charge bail.

[3] https://www.cps.gov.uk/publications/directors_guidance/dpp_guidance_5.html accessed on 26 August 2017.

[4] http://www.cps.gov.uk/legal/h_to_k/honour_based_violence_and_forced_marriage accessed on 26 August 2016.

[5] HMCPSI, HMIC, Joint Inspection on the Provision of Charging Decisions, (May 2015).

[6] The Director's Guidance on Charging (2013) is issued under the provisions of Section 37A of the Police and Criminal Evidence Act 1984 (PACE) and sets out arrangements prescribed by the Director of Public

Code for Crown Prosecutors and the content of Charging Reports and the National File Standard.

Prosecuting Counsel

Where cases proceed to trial at Crown Court, the selection of prosecuting counsel requires careful consideration. Consideration should be given to the level of experience of counsel selected, and whether they have knowledge and understanding of culturally driven offending. Whilst specially ticketed (accreditation) counsel is used by the CPS for cases involving rape and serious sexual offences, this currently does not extend to cases of FGM, forced marriage and honour-based violence/abuse. The authors believe that given the complex nature of such offences, similar tickets would assist those prosecuting such cases.

Expert Witnesses

Expert witnesses are important in prosecuting harmful traditional practice cases. For example, medical evidence may be central to providing evidence of FGM, or an expert with knowledge of a harmful traditional practice may be needed to explain its characteristics or motivation to the court.

In common law, there is a general rule that witnesses must state facts, not opinions. There are effectively two exceptions to this general rule: certain types of evidence given by non-expert witnesses (see later in this chapter) and the evidence given by expert witnesses.

An expert witness is a witness who provides the court with a statement of opinion on any admissible matter related to their expertise. Expert witnesses must be appropriately qualified and/or experienced in the matters in question to give an opinion. The general rule is that expert witnesses should only testify in relation to matters within their knowledge, not opinion or belief. However, exceptions have been made by statute and under common law in relation to expert evidence. The Criminal Justice Act 1988 states that an expert's report

---

Prosecutions for the joint working of police officers and prosecutors during the investigation and prosecution of criminal cases. It replaces all earlier editions and incorporates the National File Standard. See, https://www.cps.gov.uk/publications/directors_guidance/dpp_guidance_5.html accessed on 26 August 2017.

is admissible as evidence of fact and opinion, whether or not the expert attends court to give oral evidence.[7]

An expert witness can rely on published and unpublished material in reaching conclusions, draw on his or her own experience and that of colleagues, and may refer to research papers, learned articles and letters during the course of giving testimony, such documents being themselves admitted in evidence and supporting any inferences which can fairly be drawn from them.

Care must be taken in selecting an appropriate expert and this relates to the specific needs and context of the case. It is particularly important to be clear about the purpose of the expert testimony. For example, is the expert evidence designed to provide survivor experience? Is the expert a specialist providing cultural context? Or is the expert a medical specialist who can date and identify whether or not abuse has taken place and if so, what type? In this regard, there are two broad types of expert witness that have been used in the UK in harmful traditional practice trials. These are *medical experts* and *cultural experts*.

Medical Expert Witnesses

Medical expert witnesses are usually individuals who are medically qualified and have specific knowledge and experience of harmful traditional practices. They may, for example, be able to comment upon and interpret the source of a victim's injuries, perhaps being able to state that a set of injuries were consistent with FGM.

There is however an acknowledge dearth of medically trained experts in harmful traditional practices. The lack of medical expertise in FGM was illustrated in the UK's first criminal trial for an FGM offence. Here the medical witnesses' knowledge of FGM was rigorously tested. Similarly, the lack of experts was emphasised in Sir James Munby's judgement in a case of FGM, B & G (Children) (2), in January 2015, where he stated,

There is a dearth of medical experts in this area, particularly in relation to FGM in young children. Specific training and education, is highly desirable.[8]

The need for appropriate training of medical experts is therefore of fundamental importance. This is particularly so since, as one might expect, expert

---

[7] Criminal Justice Act 1988, Section 30.
[8] B and G (Children) (No 2) [2015] EWFC 3 at79 (i).

evidence is challenged rigorously and meticulously in court through cross-examination and the application of the Criminal Procedure Rules.

The authors argue that it is therefore of some importance that more medical specialists be trained in the examination of victims and survivors of harmful traditional practices. As many are children, this would be particularly appropriate for specialists working within paediatrics. More broadly, training in how to provide evidence in criminal and civil judicial proceedings would also be useful.

Where expertise is lacking domestically, it is possible to obtain appropriate experts from overseas although this will have a consequent impact on the cost of proceedings.

Cultural Experts

There are a number of academics and campaigners who can be classified as cultural experts. These are individuals with specialist knowledge of harmful traditional practices and may be able to comment upon issues such as why a particular practice takes place, and distinguish between the cultural and regional variations in presentation. As with medical experts, it is possible to obtain cultural experts from overseas.

The use of cultural experts, including those who come from overseas, was demonstrated in the first trial for the murder of Tulay Goren. During the investigation, investigators travelled to Kurdistan where Tulay and her family originated to better understand honour and honour codes. Turkish psychiatric experts were then engaged as expert witnesses in the UK trial.[9]

The use of cultural expert evidence can be particularly useful in trying to understand and explain the concepts of honour and shame to a court. This is because, as we have seen in previous chapters (especially Chap. 2 on honour-based abuse), an understanding of these concepts is highly relevant to motive in cases of abuse related to harmful traditional practices.

There is precedence for this in international courts. In Canada, the prosecution used the concept of 'honour' to show pre-meditation in relation to a murder allegation. In May 2009 Hasibullah Sadiqi, 23-years old, was convicted of murdering his sister, 20-year old Khatera Sadiqi and her fiancé Feroz Mangal, aged 23 years. The Sadiqi and Mangal families both originated from Afghanistan but were from different cultural backgrounds. The Sadiqi family are Tajik while the Mangals are Pashtun. The accused told the court he wanted

---

[9] https://www.theguardian.com/uk/2009/dec/17/tulay-goren-father-honour-killing accessed on 25 April 2020.

his sister to show greater respect for their father and became angry when Mr Mangal did not support him on this point. The prosecution successfully argued that the killing was an honour killing, sparked by anger over the couple's engagement.

The Duties of an Expert Witness

Expert witnesses have a number of duties that are detailed within Rule 19.2 and 19.4 of the Criminal Procedures Act. These set out duties such as experts defining their area of expertise and what the contents of their report should entail. Experts instructed by the prosecution are expected to have regard to the National Police Chiefs' Council (NPCC)] (formerly known as the Association of Chief Police Officers)/CPS Guidance for Experts,[10] which sets out their obligations in relation to case management and disclosure. Forensic Science providers must also comply with Core Foundation Principles. Streamlined forensic reporting and summaries of evidence should be used where applicable, to ensure that expert evidence is presented as simply as possible, court time is saved and unnecessary forensic work is avoided.

Non-expert Witnesses

A non-expert witness is allowed to express an opinion or impression where the facts perceived are too complicated or too evanescent in their nature to be recollected or separately and distinctly narrated. Some examples of matters on which a non-expert witness may state an opinion are:

1. estimations of speed and distance;
2. the identity of persons or articles;
3. the state of the weather;
4. the condition of articles and
5. the age of persons or articles.

Many of these are considerations within cases relevant to harmful traditional practices and prosecutors should be alive to the potential use of such witnesses. In this context non-expert witnesses may provide details that may be relevant to broader cultural and situational issues surrounding abuse.

---

[10] www.cps.gov.uk/legal/assets/uploads/files/expert_evidence_first_edition_2014.pdf accessed on 3 March 2017.

Court Procedure and Managing the Victim

Victims and survivors of harmful traditional practices may be reluctant or otherwise have difficulties attending court and giving evidence due to their age, personal circumstances, fear of intimidation, threats to kill, direct or indirect witness intimidation or other needs. It is important not to under-estimate the immense courage it takes for victims and survivors to report to police, participate in criminal investigations and provide evidence in criminal judicial proceedings. The accused and their supporters may even try every 'trick in the book' to prevent them from giving evidence at court.

Special Measures in the Criminal Courts

Special measures introduced by the Youth Justice and Criminal Evidence Act exist in the criminal courts to assist vulnerable and intimidated witnesses to give their best evidence in court by relieving some of the stresses associated with giving evidence.[11] Fear can also affect the quantity and quality of communication with, and by, witnesses of all ages. This is likely for harmful traditional practice cases. In the case of harmful traditional practices, fear often stems from the witness's experience of threats to kill or threats of other serious crimes against them, or other psychological ploys to prevent them giving evidence. For example, there has been a case of the victim's family sitting with the defendant's family in court in view of the witness.

Special measures are witness specific. A witness's eligibility for special measures, regardless of the offence, is subject to the discretion of the court and does not mean that the court will automatically grant them. The court has to satisfy itself that the special measure or combination of special measures is likely to maximise the quality of the witness's evidence before granting an application.

The Youth Justice and Criminal Evidence Act 1999 Part II

This act introduced a range of measures that can be used to facilitate the gathering and giving of evidence by vulnerable and intimidated witnesses in the criminal courts.[12] We argue that the family courts would benefit from the introduction of analogous provisions.

---

[11] Criminal Justice and Youth Evidence Act 1999, Section 19.
[12] Criminal Justice and Youth Evidence Act 1999, Sections 23–30.

Vulnerable witnesses are defined by the Youth Justice and Criminal Evidence Act (YJCEA), Section 16 as[13]:

- All child witnesses (under 18), and
- Any witness whose quality of evidence is likely to be diminished because they -

  - are suffering from a mental disorder (as defined by the Mental Health Act 1983);
  - have a significant impairment of intelligence and social functioning; or
  - have a physical disability or are suffering from a physical disorder.

- Intimidated witnesses defined by the YJCEA, Section 17 as

  those suffering from fear or distress in relation to testifying in the case.[14]

Complainants in sexual offences are defined by Section 17(4) as automatically falling into the intimidated witness category unless they wish to opt out. This is also so for witnesses to certain offences involving guns and knives. Victims/survivors of HBA, FGM, forced marriage, racially motivated crime and repeat victimisation, the families of homicide victims, witnesses who self-neglect/self-harm, or who are elderly and/or frail might also be regarded as intimidated.

While the YJCEA distinguishes between vulnerable and intimidated witnesses in respect of the criteria for their eligibility for special measures, it is important to remember that some witnesses may be vulnerable as well as intimidated, other witnesses may be vulnerable but not subject to intimidation, and others may not be vulnerable but may be subject to intimidation. It is therefore important not to attempt to categorise witnesses too rigidly.

The special measures available to vulnerable and intimidated witnesses, with the agreement of the court, include[15]:

- Screens may be made available to shield the witness from the defendant.[16]
- Live link: a live video link enables the witness to give evidence during the trial from outside the court through a televised link to the courtroom. The

---

[13] http://www.legislation.gov.uk/ukpga/1999/23/contents accessed on 27 August 2017.
[14] Ibid.
[15] Ibid.
[16] Section 23 Youth Justice and Criminal Evidence Act (YJCEA)1999.

witness may be accommodated either within the court building, or in a suitable location outside the court.[17]

- Evidence given in private (available for some vulnerable and intimidated witnesses): exclusion from the court of members of the public and the press (except for one named person to represent the press) in cases involving sexual offences or intimidation by someone other than the accused.[18]

- Removal of wigs and gowns (available for vulnerable and intimidated witnesses at the Crown Court): removal of wigs and gowns by judges and barristers.[19]

- Video-recorded interview: a video-recorded interview with a vulnerable or intimidated witness before the trial may be admitted by the court as the witness's evidence-in-chief. For adult complainants in sexual offence trials in the Crown Court a video recorded interview will be automatically admissible upon application unless this would not be in the interests of justice or would not maximise the quality of the complainant's evidence. The Coroners and Justice Act 2009, s 103 relaxes the restrictions on a witness giving additional evidence in chief after the witness's video-recorded interview has been admitted. Video-recorded cross examination has been tested at Leeds, Liverpool and Kingston Crown Courts.[20]

- Examination of the witness through an intermediary (available for vulnerable witnesses): an intermediary may be appointed by the court to assist the witness to give their evidence at court. They can also provide communication assistance in the investigation stage approval for admission of evidence so taken is then sought retrospectively. The intermediary is allowed to explain questions or answers, so far as is necessary, to enable them to be understood by the witness or the questioner but without changing the substance of the evidence.[21]

- Aids to communication (available for vulnerable witnesses): these may be permitted to enable a witness to give best evidence whether through a communicator or interpreter, or through a communication aid or technique, provided that the communication can be independently verified and understood by the court.[22]

---

[17] (YJCEA) 1999 Section 24.
[18] (YJCEA) 1999 Section 25.
[19] (YJCEA) 1999 Section 26.
[20] (YJCEA) 1999 Section 28.
[21] (YJCEA) 1999 Section 27.
[22] (YJCEA) 1999 Section 30.

In addition to special measures, the YJCEA 1999 also contains the following other provisions:

- Mandatory protection of witness from cross-examination by the accused in person: a prohibition on an unrepresented defendant from cross-examining vulnerable child and adult victims and survivors in certain classes of cases involving sexual offences.
- Discretionary protection of witness from cross-examination by the accused in person: in other types of offence, the court has a discretion to prohibit an unrepresented defendant from cross-examining the victim in person.
- Restrictions on evidence and questions about complainant's sexual behaviour: The Act restricts the circumstances in which the defence can bring evidence about the sexual behaviour of a complainant in cases of rape and other sexual offences.
- Reporting restrictions: The Act provides for restrictions on reporting by the media of information likely to lead to the identification of certain adult witnesses in criminal proceedings.

Applications for Special Measures in Criminal Cases

The process for the application of special measures is clear and well-rehearsed in the criminal courts and can assist victims/survivors and witnesses in such cases.

The first contact with victims/survivors and witnesses is through the police service. The College of Policing Guidance to police investigators states that 'investigators should consider *Ministry of Justice (2015) Code of Practice for Victims of Crime* when setting the victim and witness strategy.'[23] Three interdependent strategies make up the victim and witness strategy in an investigation—namely the witness identification, initial contact and witness interview strategies. The authors would contend that there is a fourth strategy that relates to risk management and support including support through the justice process. The investigator is required to make an initial assessment of the witness prior to conducting an interview. This assessment is necessary to determine whether the category of vulnerable or intimidated witness applies.

The Ministry of Justice, *Achieving Best Evidence in Criminal Proceedings Guidance*, provides investigators with advice on conducting a witness assessment, which should include their availability to attend court, the need for

---

[23] https://www.app.college.police.uk/app-content/investigations/victims-and-witnesses/#victim-and-witness-support accessed on 4 March 2017.

specific assistance and the need for support as a vulnerable or intimidated witness.[24] In addition, the assessment should include details of any information provided to the witness under local agreements.

When Is an Application Made?

Prosecutors must apply for special measures in writing to the court using the designated form as soon as reasonably practicable and, in any event, not more than 28 days after the defendant pleads not guilty in a magistrates' court or 14 days after the defendant pleads not guilty in the Crown Court. The application must be served on the court and the defence. The time limit can be extended upon application to the court, provided an explanation is given. The court will decide which, if any, of the special measures will be available for the witness.

What Considerations Are Made Prior to Making an Application?

Before any such application is made the prosecutor must have sufficient information about the witness and the wishes of the witness, particularly whether the witness actually wants to give evidence using special measures—some witnesses may prefer to give evidence without special measures.[25] The court will need to be told about any views expressed by the witness generally, and the specific views of the witness when determining who should accompany the witness if s/he gives evidence by live link.

With regard to intimidated witnesses, the YJCEA lists a number of factors that the court must take into account when assessing whether the witness qualifies for any of the special measures. The factors include:

- nature and alleged circumstances of the offence;
- age of the witness;
- social and cultural background and ethnic origins of the witness;
- any religious beliefs or political opinions of the witness;
- domestic and employment circumstances of the witness; and

---

[24] Ministry of Justice, Achieving Best Evidence in Criminal Proceedings: Guidance on interviewing victims and witnesses, and guidance on using special measures (March 2011).

[25] http://www.cps.gov.uk/legal/s_to_u/special_measures/ accessed on 27 August 2017.

- any behaviour towards the witness on the part of the accused, their family or associates, or any other witness or co-accused (this may be particularly relevant in cases of domestic violence).

It is imperative that an early discussion takes place with the lead police investigator and the prosecutor about the needs of vulnerable or intimidated witness(es) and the appropriateness of making an application to the court for special measures. Where the meeting is held prior to the prosecutor applying to the court for the special measures direction, then this is a good opportunity to confirm the views of the witness as to which of the special measures should be applied for. Where the meeting is held after the application for a special measures direction, has been granted, the purpose of the meeting will be to inform the witness of the special measures granted and the binding effect of the court's direction.

Can the Special Measures Direction be Altered or Discharged?

Special measures directions are binding until the end of the trial, although courts can alter or discharge a direction if it seems to be in the interests of justice to do so. The prosecution or the defence can apply for the direction to be altered or discharged (or the court may do so of its own motion), but must show that there has been a significant change of circumstances since the court made the direction or since an application for it to be altered was last made.

In addition to the statutory special measures, prosecutors may consider whether the witness would benefit from more informal arrangements such as pre-trial visits and having regular breaks while giving their evidence.

Child Witnesses

The original distinction in criminal cases between child witnesses in need of special protection and children giving evidence in all other types of cases no longer applies.[26] The effect of this change is to place all child witnesses in the same position regardless of the offence. For all child witnesses, there is a presumption that they will give their evidence in chief by video recorded

---

[26] Coroners and Justice Act 2009, Section 101 amending the YJCEA, Section 21.

interview and any further evidence by live link unless the court is satisfied that this will not improve the quality of the child's evidence.

However, a child witness may opt out of giving their evidence by either video recorded interview or by live link or both, subject to the agreement of the court. If the child witness opts out, then there is a presumption that they will give their evidence in court from behind a screen. Should the child witness not wish to use a screen they may also be allowed to opt out of using it, again subject to the agreement of the court. In deciding whether or not to agree to the wish of the child witness, the court must be satisfied that the quality of the child's evidence will not be diminished.

Witness Anonymity

Protection of witnesses and victims/survivors is critical in order to demonstrate support for them and to provide them with confidence and reassurance.

A court may also be requested to make a witness-anonymity order pursuant to the Coroners and Justice Act 2009, FGM Act 2003 (amended) and the Anti-social Behaviour Crime and Victims Act 2014 (amended).[27] The measures sought in relation to a witness for whom such an application is made include the following:

- His/her name and other identifying details should be withheld and removed from material disclosed to any party to the proceedings.
- He/she should use a pseudonym.
- He/she should be asked no questions that might lead to his/her identification.
- He/she should be screened from all in court other than the judge and jury.
- He/she should give evidence by remote TV link.
- His/her image should be obscured for all in court other than the judge, jury and supporter present.
- His/her voice should be electronically disguised for all in court other than the judge and jury.
- There should be a delay button so that answers given by the witness that may reveal identity can be excluded.

The Court of Appeal has held that none of the conditions have more weight than the other and the list is not exhaustive, they leave open the possibility

---

[27] Coroners and Justice Act 2009, Sections 86 and 87.

that in an individual case some further point may properly arise for consideration.

For specific applicability in HBA cases; see *R V Azhar Nazir* [2009] EWCA Crim 213 at 33–59.[28] The victim Samaira Nazir, a 26-year-old woman of Pakistani origin was killed in her family home, as she wished to marry a man her family deemed unsuitable. A witness anonymity order was made for a witness with the pseudonym Rabia Farooq who gave evidence that she witnessed the appellant brother of the deceased pulling the victim who was already injured back into the house when she was trying to escape. In the above case, a written statement from the witness stated that:

> *I am very afraid of the defendant Azhar, and that I am very much scared and worried, that if he finds out that I have given some statement in this case, he will beat and harm myself and my family members as well, I wont be able to speak up okay in the court if he is there and I'm there and I cant confront him in that manner, I don't want to go to court if he is there for the sake of my safety.*

Two items of legislation affecting anonymity have taken effect in England, Wales and Northern Ireland. The Serious Crime Act 2015, which inserted Section 4a into the Female Genital Mutilation Act 2003, and now provides the victims and survivors of FGM with lifelong anonymity from the point of making an allegation to the police (subject to any restrictions imposed by the courts).[29] Similarly, the Policing and Crime Act 2017 inserts a Section 122A into Part 10 of the Anti-social Behaviour, Crime and Policing Act 2014, which also provides victims and survivors of forced marriage lifelong anonymity from the point that she/he reports an allegation to the police.[30]

The protection of the witness during the court process as well as the ongoing future protection of the victim is also a crucial consideration involving not only the consideration of anonymity/special measures available in the court process but additionally the possible relocation of the witness as well as a change of identity. The relocation of the witness has been stated by Court of Appeal not to provide a practicable alternative to an anonymity order, as by definition, a witness would be cut off from all their roots and have to start completely new lives, as would their spouse and children. The interference with the life of any such witness would be tumultuous and would effectively penalise her/him for doing their duty as a citizen. Witness relocation can only

[28] R V Azhar *Nazir* [2009] EWCA Crim 213 Paras 33–59.
[29] Serious Crime Act, Section 71.
[30] http://www.legislation.gov.uk/ukpga/2017/3/section/173/enacted accessed on 3 September 2017.

be a practicable alternative in the rarest of circumstances and if enforced on a witness may engage his or her human right to a private life.[31]

Previous Offences

It is often the case with harmful traditional practices that the subject matter of the charge does not stand in isolation. Consideration needs therefore to be given to whether or not there is a history which has culminated in the specific offence reported. In particular, whether there have been any previous reports of violence, or any attempts by the victim to absent themselves from the family home and seek refuge elsewhere to avoid the threat of violence. Any criminal investigation and prosecution must consider the totality of offending. In the case of Shafilea Ahmed, a senior homelessness officer reported that Shafilea (who had been running away from the family home since aged 11 years) had told her she had nowhere to live and was fleeing an arranged marriage, with violence at home having escalated since she was 15 years old. In 2003, Shafilea also drank bleach whilst on a visit to Pakistan to escape being forced into a marriage. Although such a history may be relevant, careful consideration should also be given to the parameters of the admissibility of any history of violence. The demeanour of the victim as witnessed at the time of the incident will also be an important factor, in particular any distress exhibited, as well as signs of injury.

Concurrent Criminal and Civil Proceedings

In cases of harmful traditional practices, it is relatively common that there may be concurrent criminal and civil proceedings. The 2013 Protocol and Good Practice Model Disclosure of Information, in cases of alleged child abuse and linked criminal and care directions hearings, provides helpful guidance which will apply to cases involving criminal investigations into alleged child abuse[32] (child victims and survivors who were aged 17 and under at the

---

[31] See R V Mayers [2008] EWCA 2989 at para. 9.
[32] Child abuse includes both sexual abuse and non-sexual abuse.

time of the alleged offending) and/or Family Court[33] proceedings concerning a child (aged 17 and under).[34]

There is every likelihood that the number of proceedings in the family courts will increase as local authorities seek to protect children and others 'at risk' of HBA, forced marriage, CEFM, FGM and other forms of harmful cultural practice.

The Role of Civil Society Organisations

Civil society organisations have an important role to play in the context of prosecutions as well as more broadly in advocacy and victim care. These organisations often involve advisors and caseworkers who are themselves survivors of harmful traditional practices. Their experiences are invaluable and offer both police investigators and legal professionals a deep cultural insight into affected communities. We have considered some of these roles in previous chapters.

Challenges for Investigators and Prosecutors

Evidence Gathering

There are many challenges faced during the evidence gathering phase of an investigation. The age of victims and survivors is a particular challenge as many forms of harmful traditional practice are directed towards very young children, that is, children under eight years. Within this age range there is a risk that these children may be unreliable as witnesses as they may be unable to articulate or remember aspects of their experience. It is therefore vitally important that prosecutors and the police are sensitive to this and are cognisant of achieving best evidence procedures and appropriate methods of dealing with children.

As we have noted, many harmful traditional practices occur overseas. This makes collecting evidence difficult and compounds any challenges related to the age of victims and survivors. The first challenge is tracing witnesses from

---

[33] Family Court means for the time being the Family Proceedings Court, the County Court (when exercising its family jurisdiction) and the Family Division of the High Court. Once the Family Court comes into existence, it means the Family Court and the Family Division of the High Court.

[34] https://www.judiciary.gov.uk/publications/protocol-good-practice-model-2013/ accessed on 27 August 2017.

affected communities who are prepared to provide statements for prospective court. This is likely to be compounded in countries or communities where there is support for a harmful practice. In such locations there may also be a lack of support from local officials. In these circumstances, it is important to recognise that victims/survivors and witnesses may not support the investigation and/or prosecution. It is, therefore, critical for the police and prosecutors to provide the victim and any potential witnesses with culturally sensitive support and assistance. Such support and assistance is best provided by qualified public authority and civil society specialist organisations. It may take a significant amount of time, encouragement, reassurance and support to build the confidence and trust of affected community members to provide statements and other evidence as part of a criminal investigation. In overseas cases there are also other challenges including, securing appropriate medical evidence from local practitioners, obtaining immigration entry/exit clearances, and obtaining other documentary evidence.

Reluctant Witnesses

In many cases of abuse associated with harmful traditional practices it may be necessary for family members to give evidence against each other. This can be significantly challenging, for example, some individuals may be very reluctant to give evidence against a spouse or other family member. This reluctance to give evidence may be compounded for a witness who is compelled to give evidence. Therefore, the decision to compel a reluctant witness to attend court with a view to giving evidence for the prosecution should be exercised with sensitivity and discretion. Reluctant witnesses may react in a number of different ways, these might include becoming hostile refusing to give evidence so becoming in contempt of court, or may give their evidence.

There is substantial legislation surrounding the conditions where reluctant witnesses, especially spouses, may be compelled to give evidence. In cases where the victim may be required to give evidence against his or her spouse, police and prosecutors will need to consider the Police and Criminal Evidence (PACE) Act 1984, s 80.[35] Spouses or civil partners of a person charged in proceedings are generally considered competent to give evidence for the prosecution, with the only exception being if the spouse or civil partner is jointly

---

[35] This is the statutory provision which governs the competence and compellability of spouses and civil partners in criminal proceedings.

charged.[36] Spouses or civil partners are also competent and compellable to give evidence on behalf of the defendant or the defendant's co-accused.[37]

The prosecution can only compel a spouse or civil partner to give evidence for the prosecution in cases which involve:

- an allegation of violence against the spouse or civil partner,
- an allegation of violence against a person who was, at the material time, under the age of 16 years,
- an alleged sexual offence against a victim who was, at the material time, under the age of 16 years, or
- attempting, conspiring or aiding and abetting, counselling and procuring to commit the offences in the categories above.

If a spouse witness is divorced from the defendant or the civil partnership comes to an end before he or she gives evidence, the former spouse/civil partner is competent and compellable to give evidence as if that person and the accused had never been married or had never been civil partners.

Victim as a Defence Witness

In cases of harmful traditional practice, it is possible that the victim may wish to give evidence in support of the defendant, their abuser. This may happen for a variety of reasons. Often victims and survivors, especially children, may not wish to see a loved one prosecuted, they may not recognise their experience as abuse and may even be supportive of the practice. They may also be in fear of their abuser and supporting them may be a means of self-protection.

Where a victim chooses to make a statement on behalf of the defendant(s), he or she may also be required to give evidence for the defence and be subject to cross-examination by the prosecution. This happened in the UK's first trial relating to FGM.[38]

Investigators and prosecutors must be alert to the possibility that victims and survivors may not wish to support a prosecution of a family member. Accordingly, an effective strategy must be developed to manage this prospect. In these circumstances an important consideration to make is if the victim should be treated as a hostile witness. In these circumstances, it is important that evidence must be secured from the victim as soon as possible. Also,

---

[36] A witness is deemed to be competent if he or she can lawfully be called to give evidence.

[37] A witness is compellable if he or she may lawfully be required to give evidence.

[38] R V Dharmasena and Mohamed.

evidence from other evidential sources which prove, or disprove the victim's evidence must be also be secured as soon as possible.

Sentencing Guidelines

There are at present no specific sentencing guidelines for crimes related to honour-based violence/abuse, forced marriage or FGM despite there being an argument in favour of them. This is because sentencing guidelines for these offences would help achieve sentencing consistency and demonstrate how seriously such offending is viewed.

In the absence of specific guidelines, offenders will be sentenced in accordance with the existing relevant sentencing guidelines. The Sentencing Council for the UK issues definitive sentencing guidelines for application across the criminal justice system in England and Wales.[39] The minimum sentencing starting points are set out as well as the aggravating and mitigating factors to be taken into account by a sentencing court.

However, we argue that the sentencing guidelines for offences closely associated with HBA, including Murder, Grievous Bodily Harm with Intent, Assault occasioning Actual Bodily harm and Kidnapping/False Imprisonment fail to specifically reflect the unique nature of HBA offences. The unique factors within HBA often include, family-based conspiracies, the abuse of family members by other family members, abuse of a child's trust by parents, victims and survivors are often subjected to repeated violence prior to the index offence, they are often extremely vulnerable due to age and living within a close-knit community, the offending can be group-based by the community, and the violence is motivated by concerns with tradition and cultural. Although these factors are presently regarded as aggravating features in any particular case, it is true to say that the deterrent element in relation to any of those factors is unclear in the overall sentence.[40]

In the absence of specific sentencing guidelines, an examination of past sentences can only be an *indication* of the length of sentences the court should impose. The authors recommend that the Sentencing Council conducts urgent work to provide sentencing guidelines for honour-based abuse, forced marriage and female genital mutilation related crimes.

---

[39] http://www.sentencingcouncil.org.uk/wp-content/uploads/Definitive-Guideline-Imposition-of-CCS-final-web.pdf accessed on 4 March 2017.

[40] www.judiciary.gov.uk/judgments/iftikhar-ahmed-farzana-ahmed-sentencing-remarks-03082012.

Summary and Recommendations

We have considered some of the issues in prosecuting harmful traditional practices, identifying best practice where possible. However, there are a number of ongoing challenges. How are the challenges to be addressed and how can investigations and prosecutions be more effectively undertaken to the satisfaction of the victims and survivors?

Witnesses and victims/survivors of harmful traditional practices are often fearful, intimidated and vulnerable; prosecutors must have due regard to this in their approach to victims/ survivors and witnesses. Ample legislation exists to protect vulnerable and intimidated witnesses and prosecutors should make use of this so as to give support to thcm and to maintain their confidence and cooperation with court processes.

The desired outcomes of investigations and prosecutions are invariably set by the respective public authorities in accordance with policy and their respective performance regimes. Victim-focussed decision making and policies must be one of the foundations of the approach to tackling harmful traditional practices. Sustained training must also be provided for leaders and their staff within policing and the prosecution services and for expert witnesses, especially those who are medically qualified, to bolster the range of experts currently available to courts.

The approaches considered above will ensure that victims/survivors and witnesses of harmful traditional practices receive a high quality of service delivery, and that justice is both done and is seen to be done.

11

Alternative Dispute Resolution

Pressure on the UK court system has increased the use of non-judicial alternative methods of resolving disputes, such as arbitration[1] and mediation.[2] In 2008 Lord Chief Justice Phillips stated,

> there is no reason why the principles of sharia law, or any other religious code, should not be the basis for mediation or other forms of alternative dispute resolution.[3]

He went on to say,

> It must be recognised, however, that any sanctions for a failure to comply with the agreed terms of the mediation would be drawn from the laws of England and Wales.

This chapter explores alternative dispute resolution systems in the context of harmful traditional practices. It will focus upon the operation of religious arbitration through the Islamic Shari'a Councils and the Jewish Beth Din, highlighting particularly some of the current difficulties these systems have in operating alongside the UK legal system. We will consider the issue of equal justice, forced religious marriages that have not been registered in accordance

---

[1] Arbitration is where two or more parties agree an independent person who will decide their dispute, with a decision which is usually final and binding, and can be enforced by the UK courts under the Arbitration Act 1996.

[2] Mediation is voluntary and involves a neutral facilitator trying to help two or more parties to a dispute reach common ground—a mutually satisfactory agreement between the parties. This agreement can sometimes be put before the court.

[3] https://www.theguardian.com/uk/2008/jul/04/law.islam accessed on 16 September 2017.

© The Author(s) 2020
G. Campbell et al., *Harmful Traditional Practices*,
https://doi.org/10.1057/978-1-137-53312-8_11

with English Law and the role played by the Shari'a Councils and Beth Din in divorce resolution.

The reader may wonder why we have included a chapter on alternative dispute resolution in a book focussing on harmful traditional practices. Alternative religious dispute resolution provides an often used and important avenue for members of religious communities to resolve differences particularly in the sphere of marriage and divorce. However, due to a lack of overall governance and legislative control of their activities and the fact that bodies such as Shari'a courts and the Beth Din are male dominated, their behaviour and judgements can lead, either intentionally or unintentionally, to the unfair treatment of women. As some of these women could be the subject of honour-based abuse, forced marriage and domestic abuse, these courts through some of their decisions could inadvertently allow the continuance of harmful cultural practices.

Shari'a Law, Courts and Councils

What Is Shari'a Law?

Muslim law or 'the Shari'a' (which literally means 'a path to a watering place', Doi 1984:3) provides an overarching framework of values and rules relating to all aspects of life for Muslim people. Subjects covered range from religious observance to the norms of family life.[4] More broadly the Islamic legal system embodies a distinct preference for alternative methods of dispute resolution, like mediation and reconciliation. This is reflected in the traditional Islamic concept of *sulh*, which traditionally means 'amicable or peaceful settlement'.

Muslim law derives from two principal sources, the Qur'an and the Sunna. The Qur'an is the revealed scripture, and founding document, of Islam. According to the Islamic faith, the Qur'an is the uncreated word of God, believed to have been revealed, word for word, in the Arabic language through [the] Prophet Muhammad.

The *Sunnah* refers to the traditions of the Prophet Muhammad, including his teachings, practices, parables and sayings, which are contained within records called the books of 'Hadith'. The *Sunnah* is a body of work formed out of traditional stories transmitted from the Prophet Muhammed, called Hadiths. The Hadiths provide guidance to Muslims on the words and deeds

---

[4] Dr Samia Bano, An Exploratory Study of Shariah Councils in England with Respect to Family Law 2 October 2012.

of the Prophet. For Muslim scholars the Hadiths set out in the *Sunnah* provide a guide to understanding the Qur'an by passing on the teachings of the Prophet Mohammad as demonstrated by his words and conduct throughout his lifetime [c.570–632 CE].

The principles generally come in two forms, known as *ibadat* and *mu'amalat* respectively. Covering matters like prayer, fasting, and pilgrimage, *ibadat* principles address an individual's responsibilities to God (which in Arabic literally means 'worship' or 'service to God'), while *mu'amalat* principles govern matters of human interaction referring broadly to civil, commercial and procedural rules and duties like marriage, divorce, inheritance and theft.

The collective efforts of Islamic legal scholars has generated consensus on many issues and this has provided another source of Islamic law, known as *Ijma*.[5] Akin to *prior precedent* in the common law tradition, *Ijma* represents settled law with binding authority.[6] Thus, when deciding a dispute, an Islamic jurist, or *kadi*, must investigate whether the issue in question is settled by *Ijma*.[7] If the matter is conclusively resolved by *Ijma*, the *kadi* must adhere to the established rule.[8]

The final major source of Islamic law is analogical reasoning, known as *Qiyas*.[9] *Qiyas* offers a means of extending the Qur'an, the *Sunnah*, and the *Ijma* to novel matters not explicitly covered in their texts. As an accepted authoritative source, *Qiyas* must be distinguished from independent legal reasoning and problem solving, known as *Ijtihad*—a controversial issue among the different schools of Islamic legal thought.[10]

The Shari'a Councils

There is no single authoritative definition of the term 'Shari'a Council'.[11] Currently the Shari'a Councils are unofficial legal bodies, which provide advice and assistance on Muslim family law matters. Their main functions are mediation and reconciliation, issuing Muslim divorce certificates and providing expert opinion reports on issues of family law or custom. In practice,

---

[5] Muhammad Razi, Encyclopaedia of Islamic Jurisprudence 95 (2007).
[6] Ibid.
[7] Ibid.
[8] Ibid.
[9] Ibid.
[10] William Montgomery Watt, Islamic Fundamentalism 106–07 (1989).
[11] Dr Samia Bano, An Exploratory Study of Shariah Councils in England with Respect to Family Law 2 October 2012.

Shari'a Councils deal overwhelmingly with matrimonial problems,[12] but have no real powers in English Law.[13] They operate under the Arbitration Act 1996, which allows consenting adults to resolve disputes and conflicts, both civil and commercial as long as this does not conflict with UK law.[14]

Shari'a Council members include religious scholars and are presided over mainly by men. The absence of women in this process is noteworthy and has led to the development of practices that are disproportionately in favour of men.

There is a UK wide national network of 10 bodies run by the Islamic Shari'a Council in Leyton, East London. This grew out of a national conference in Birmingham in 1982, at which it was hoped to generate a single, umbrella body, whose members could with good grounds claim to represent the five schools of Sunni jurisprudence.[15]

The Birmingham Shari'a Council grew out of a women's crisis centre run by Dr Wageha Syeda, a Muslim woman and community paediatrician. Many of the women who came to her were seeking a divorce. In 2005 she asked the Birmingham Central Mosque to sponsor a council that could oversee Islamic divorce. Dr Syeda is an advisor to the Council on the cases that come before it and women are involved in clerking and presiding of this Council.[16]

The Moslem Arbitration Tribunal (MAT) offers a dispute resolution service in a number of areas of civil law and provides legally binding decisions. The MAT was established in 2007 and is part of a Sufi network in the UK inspired by the late pir or Sufi saint Shaykh Allama Muhammed Abdul Wahab Siddiqi. The MAT was founded by Siddiqi's son and its original emphasis was on commercial disputes, which in English law can be subjected by the parties themselves to binding arbitration. More recently it has come to advise couples on Islamic divorce, although divorce in English law cannot be subjected by the parties themselves to binding arbitration. The MAT always has a barrister or solicitor of England and Wales sitting as part of the tribunal, and also includes a 'Scholar of Islamic Sacred Law'.[17]

---

[12] Myriam   Francois-Cerrah,   17   July   2014   http://www.telegraph.co.uk/women/womens-politics/10973009/Sharia-courts-ban-would-harm-British-Muslim-women.html Leyton's Sharia Council in London states 95% of its cases are matrimonial problems, the majority stemming from women seeking divorce.

[13] Patrick Worrall Fact Check Q and A: sharia law in the UK 14 July 2014.

[14] Myriam   Francois-Cerrah,   17   July   2014   http://www.telegraph.co.uk/women/womens-politics/10973009/Sharia-courts-ban-would-harm-British-Muslim-women.html.

[15] Robin Griffin-Jones. 'The 'Unavoidable' Adoption of Shari'a Law' Islam and English Law Rights, Responsibilities and the Place of Shari'a.

[16] Ibid.

[17] MAT, Procedure Rules of Arbitration Tribunal, see http://www.matribunal.com/rules.php (Rule 10) as at 25 June 2016.

Use of Islamic Law

A growing number of British Muslims are turning to traditional Islamic law and Shari'a Councils to settle matrimonial disputes, issues of forced marriage and divorce, and cases involving matters of apostasy and domestic violence.[18] Importantly, the grant of a 'religious divorce' can only ever be accomplished by a religious tribunal, since a civil court can only terminate a civil marriage. That is why some Muslims may go to a Shari'a Council for a termination of their marriage. Research conducted at Cardiff University into religious tribunals found that the reason people of faith go to such bodies is to receive confirmation of their marital status, and most crucially, the licence to remarry within their religion, without which many would refuse to contemplate another marriage.[19] The religious tribunals in the Cardiff Study very clearly recognised and advised those using them that they could not give binding rulings on matters within the jurisdiction of the civil courts, and thus while they might respond to the parties' requests to engage in mediation or arbitration on finances or arrangements for their children, these would have to be endorsed by the family courts through a consent order for them to be legally enforceable.

Recognition of Shari'a Law

The acknowledgement that a parallel religious dispute resolution mechanism is in operation has heightened the debate for some recognition of Shari'a law in the UK.[20] However, there have been some concerns raised about how Shari'a councils are composed and how Shari'a law is applied. For example, concerns have been raised about the male domination of the councils and how this can lead to the application of Shari'a law that at times disadvantages women, and about some of the messaging from these councils concerning the way 'women are told to live'.[21,22] When it comes to the issue of divorce there is gender inequality within Shari'a law. Divorce may be instituted unilaterally

---

[18] Dr Samia Bano An Exploratory Study of Shariah Councils in England with Respect to Family Law 2 October 2012.

[19] Social Cohesion and Civil Law: Marriage, Divorce and Religious Courts, funded by the Arts and Humanities Research Council.

[20] Theresa May then Home Secretary Conservative Party Conference 2014.

[21] Stephen Schwartz Sharia Comes for the Archbishop 25 February 2008, *The Weekly Standard* http://www.weeklystandard.com/article/15852 accessed 23 June 2016.

[22] Islam and English Law, Rights Responsibilities and the Place of Shari'a, edited by Robin Griffith Jones 2013.

by the husband, the most common means being *ṭalāq*.[23] The wife, on the other hand, must petition for *khula*, which literally means 'extraction', or release from the marriage, and if the husband refuses her request she may petition the Shari'a Council to overrule his refusal.

Challenges

In theory, arbitration based on Shari'a law should be fairly well regulated in the UK because it takes place under the Arbitration Act. However, the absence of any other state regulation of Shari'a councils presents a number of challenges. Indeed, Muslim women are currently forced to choose between secular law and Islamic law and there is a conflict between human rights provisions on gender equality and traditional interpretations of Islamic law. Some of the challenges of parallel systems and of the risks to women were revealed in a recent case. In February 2016 the Family Division of the High Court ruled against a man who claimed that because the marriage was conducted under Shari'a, his wife, who has both British and Pakistani nationality, had to travel to Pakistan to pursue the divorce.[24] Justice Francis rejected his arguments and said that,

> It would be racial discrimination because what is said is that because the wife has dual nationality, both British and Pakistani, that as a national of Pakistan she should be treated differently from a British citizen who is not a national of Pakistan.

The judge added that it was 'clear' that,

> the rights granted to men in Pakistan to secure divorces pursuant to the laws of that country are different from the rights granted to women and that it is more onerous for a woman to secure a divorce in Pakistan than it is for a man.

If he accepted the man's claims, Justice Francis said it would mean the woman would be 'subjected to different rules of English law than people of other faiths or other nationalities living here'.

Better protection of Muslim women could be achieved by state regulation of Islamic arbitration. If the Shari'a Councils became a *forum* for arbitration under the Arbitration Act 1996, the State would have an opportunity to

---

[23] Oxford English Dictionary definition—(in Islamic law) divorce effected by the husband's enunciation of the word 'ṭalāq', this constituting a formal repudiation of his wife.
[24] B V L [2016] EWFC 67.

regulate the administering of Islamic law, particularly compliance with human rights and gender equality policies. However, forcing Shari'a Councils to abide by rules of gender equality may be considered by some to be an unjustifiable limitation of their right to religious freedom.

The Beth Din (Bateui Din): House of Judgement

Alternative dispute resolution is also a key feature of the Jewish faith. Jewish Rabbinical Courts, the Beth Din, have a long history in the UK having operated in some form or another since the time of Oliver Cromwell.[25] The Beth Din in the UK is operated by individual branches of the Jewish community, with its respective rabbinic authority interpreting Jewish Law. The best known is the London Beth Din, or the court of the Chief Rabbi, the oldest Jewish Court in the UK established in the eighteenth century.

The Beth Din are composed of three Rabbinic *dayanim* or judges. They have traditionally been concerned with the interpretation of Talmudic Law (especially religious rulings). In recent times this has expanded to include civil arbitration as an alternative to court action.[26]

Like Shari'a courts, the jurisdiction of the Beth Din in relation to civil matters is derived from the Arbitration Act 1996, which allows all British citizens to resolve civil disputes through arbitration, decisions becoming legally binding when approved by the civil courts. It is important to emphasise that it has no jurisdiction whatsoever in relation to criminal offences.

Beth Din decisions regarding costs and payment are all legally enforceable by leave of the High Court or County Court in the same manner as a judgment or order of the court to the same effect. Any agreement reached under the 1996 Act can be reviewed and overturned by the UK's civil courts, particularly where there is conflict between applicable Jewish law as applied by the Beth Din and existing UK jurisprudence.

Use of Beth Din

The Beth Din are often used when a religious divorce is sought by members of Jewish communities in addition to a civil divorce. This is because the civil divorce certificate is not considered sufficient to dissolve a Jewish marriage.

---

[25] Haim Hermann Cohn, Isacc Levitats, & Moshe Drori, Bet Din and Judges, in Encyclopaedia Judaica 512, 513 (Vol. 3 2nd ed. 2007).

[26] Pursuant to the Arbitration Act 1996.

This has important implications for Jewish couples where at least one of them is a divorcee, who wishes to marry in an orthodox synagogue. To do so they must produce evidence of both a civil and religious divorce. Evidence of the religious divorce comes from having a 'Get' certificate or writ of divorce. The 'Get' is the instrument of divorce. A 'Get' can only be obtained with the consent of both parties in a religious divorce, and this is commonly used as a bargaining tool in ancillary matters. Failure to produce this means that they will be considered still to be married to their previous partner (even if they can prove civil divorce) and will be regarded as committing adultery.[27]

Jewish divorce law differs from a civil divorce in two ways. Firstly, a Jewish divorce cannot be imposed on an unwilling spouse by either their partner or the Beth-Din, only spouses with mutual agreement can give and accept a 'Get'. Indeed, the Beth-Din will only entertain Jewish Divorce proceedings when approached by two consenting parties. Secondly, unlike the Civil grounds for divorce in the UK, where a decree nisi/absolute can only be granted if one of five specified grounds are proven, there is no requirement in the Beth Din to claim any particular grounds for a divorce. The Beth Din, in contrast to the Shari'a Council, play the role of referee once the formalities of a consensual exit from the marriage have been complied with, they do not undo a marriage.

Once a religious divorce is declared it is not uncommon for the other party to contest its validity.[28] For instance, an Orthodox Jew may contest the validity of a religious divorce pronounced by a Beth Din, which does not conform to Orthodox Judaism. In such circumstances one or both parties might adduce expert evidence to determine whether the religious divorce is valid according to religious usages. The stay of a decree absolute will continue until the court is satisfied by a declaration by both parties that the marriage is also dissolved in accordance with Jewish usages. Once a valid religious divorce has been granted, an English court will pronounce a decree absolute and the parties will be divorced according to both religious law and English law.

Impact of Refusal of a *Get*

There are a number of negative implications where one partner refuses to comply with an application for a 'Get'. Without a 'Get' a wife has the status of *Agunah* or chained woman. She is prohibited from remarrying in an

---

[27] David Frei, Issues to consider when Jewish and Muslim women seek a divorce, 29 June 2017 at the Supreme Court.
[28] Ibid., Section 10A (4).

Orthodox synagogue. If she re-marries in the civil courts without a 'Get' she will be regarded as adulterous and any future child of hers will be considered a *mamzer* in Jewish Law. This has important social and religious consequences in that the child would not be able to marry in an Orthodox synagogue.

The consequences for a man whose wife refused to accept a 'Get' are less far-reaching. Although he will remain married in the eyes of the Orthodox community (known as an *Agun*) and is also not permitted to re-marry in an Orthodox synagogue, if he has a child with another Jewish woman his child will be considered *halakhically* Jewish (Jewish according to Jewish Law) as long as, at the time of conception, the mother is unmarried and the legitimate child of a Jewish mother.

The refusal of the 'Get' is regarded as a form of domestic or psychological abuse, attempting to control the life of a former spouse. In extreme cases, it is a form of blackmail in order to obtain financial concessions in ancillary proceedings. In response the London Beth Din has started to impose sanctions on those husbands who refuse their wives a 'Get'. In November 2016 the London Beth-Din issued an advertisement in the case of John Abayahoudayan, who had refused to grant his wife Rivkah a 'Get' for 15 years. This urged Mr Abayahoudayan to *do what is proper according to Jewish law and morality and release Rivkah from being an agunah.* In another case, Yossi Elkouby, was called upon to appear before the Beth Din and to comply with its instructions to give a 'Get'. Until he had complied fully, the *Harchakos d'Rabbeinu Tam* was invoked and the community in London and Paris (where he was thought to be residing) were called upon to refuse him entry to all *Shuls*, synagogues, and consider the appropriateness of any social or economic interactions with him. This is in line with The Rabbinical courts law and with the Chief Rabbi being determined to minimise and eradicate such abuses, so that women are able to move on with their lives when the marriage is clearly over.[29]

As 'Get' refusal is becoming more common, pre-nuptial agreements, enforceable by civil law, are making provision for 'Get' refusal in the event of a divorce. These ensure that in the event of a divorce, the Beth Din will have the proper authority to ensure that the 'Get' is not used as a bargaining chip.

The Divorce (Religious Marriages) Act 2002 gave the civil courts the power to refuse a civil decree absolute until a religious divorce had been obtained. This was designed to prevent individuals who used a religious marriage as a bargaining tool in divorce proceedings.

---

[29] Enforcement of Divorce Judgements 5755-1995 Law Book of the State of Israel.

Religious Arbitration and the Principles of English Law

We have considered two commonly used forms of religious arbitration, Shari'a courts and the Beth Din. We have noted that each is used often in matrimonial divorce cases to affect a religious divorce. We have noted that whilst these courts have important functions within their respective communities, there are potential problems. In both cases there is potential for the rights of women to be compromised, either unintentionally due to the make-up of the courts or intentionally by using their processes to limit a woman's freedom. In addition, there is a possibility for courts or their members to make misleading statements about the legal status of their rulings and the courts may at times provide rulings that can be at variance with UK laws.

In the context of harmful traditional practices such as forced marriage and other abuse, these issues are highly relevant. A religious court's rulings, that may be consistent with scriptural interpretations, could in principle serve to prolong abuse by failing to grant a religious divorce.

Legislative responses to these challenges can close legal loopholes and would protect the rights of women and more clearly specify the place of religious courts within the criminal justice system. Baroness Cox has introduced a Bill into the UK House of Lords that is designed to meet some of these challenges. This Private Members' Bill is supported by the National Secular Society (NSS), 'all party' and Muslim women's groups and other organisations concerned with the suffering of vulnerable women. The Bill is intended to tackle discrimination suffered by women in religious courts. The Bill, which applies to all arbitration tribunals, especially outlaws the common practice of these courts of giving a woman's testimony half the weight to that of a man's and addresses various human rights issues.

The Bill's proposals include:

1. A new criminal offence of 'falsely claiming legal jurisdiction' for any person who adjudicates upon matters which ought to be decided by criminal or family courts. The maximum penalty would be five years in prison. This is designed to prevent religious courts overstating their jurisdiction and powers.
2. Explicitly states that sex discrimination law applies directly to arbitration tribunal proceedings. Discriminatory rulings may be struck down under the Bill.

3. Requires public bodies to inform women that they have fewer legal rights if their marriage is unrecognised in English law.
4. Explicitly states that arbitration tribunals may not deal with matters of family law (such as a *legally* recognised divorce or custody of children) or criminal law (such as domestic law).
5. Makes it easier for a civil court to set aside a consent order if a mediation settlement agreement or other agreement was reached under duress.
6. Explicitly states in the legislation that a victim of domestic abuse is a witness to an offence, and therefore should be expressly protected from witness intimidation.

Thus, if a Beth Din, or a Shari'a Council, were to suggest an outcome, so much at odds with English law as to cast doubt on its fairness or to raise concerns about the welfare of any children involved, no English court would give it effect. Insofar as such a body makes a determination that is in accordance with English law, there is no reason not to give it effect and indeed, every reason to do so, since it would also be squarely in line with current policy and practice to encourage the parties to find a resolution without taking up the time and resources of the civil courts. However, the passage of the bill was stopped as a result of the contentious prorogation of the 2017–2019 Parliamentary session.

Summary and Recommendations

We have considered the characteristics, strengths and challenges presented by religious courts as modes of alternative dispute resolution. We have noted that they can and do provide important opportunities for communities to resolve disputes in line with their religious beliefs. However, the characteristics of the courts and the dearth of regulation governing them mean that there are challenges that most frequently negatively impact women and girls and that can, often inadvertently, allow the continuance of harmful traditional practices. Whilst religious courts are community led, they are not at present part of community driven solutions to harmful traditional practices, resting as they do on tradition and male dominance, they could be seen as part of the problem reinforcing the inequitable treatment of women.

Alternative Dispute Resolution, which operates in accordance with UK law, has an important role to play. However, the authors contend that additional checks and balances are required to protect those who appear before Shari'a Councils or Beth Dins. This can only be achieved through clear and consistent legislation, and the appointment of a diverse panel of judges including men, women and independent panel members drawn both from inside and outside of the faith. In addition, the introduction of an appeals process where there is equitable treatment would also send a clear message to those who preside over cases that their decisions are subject to scrutiny and must be fair, equitable and non-discriminatory. If this were to happen then these courts could provide a valuable community-based challenge to some of the harmful traditional practices discussed in this book.

12

Overview and Conclusions

In the pages of this book, we have discussed a diverse range of harmful traditional practices. We have examined the characteristics of these practices, their impact and considered responses to them in terms of prevention, legislation, investigation and prosecution. Whilst much work has been done to date to establish legislative frameworks, collaborative working and awareness raising amongst professionals, there remains a significant gap in the knowledge and experience of professionals across a range of disciplines concerning harmful traditional practices that has led to a number of challenges. As we have highlighted, these challenges include the following:

1. Difficulties in recognising harmful traditional practices resulting from professionals missing warning signs or misclassifying behaviours.
2. Failures to report cases often as required by legislation.
3. Inadequate prevalence data resulting from failures to report cases, leading to limited knowledge about true rates of offending.
4. Inappropriate responses to victims and survivors failing to provide adequate protection or presenting them with poor advice and support, inadvertently increasing the risk of harm.
5. Failures in multiagency working through failing to see the importance of multiagency work in this area, or through failures to develop adequate joint working practices.
6. Failures in sustained proactive engagement by public authorities with affected communities.
7. Failures in investigations and prosecutions leading to relatively few (successful) prosecutions for harmful traditional practices.

© The Author(s) 2020
G. Campbell et al., *Harmful Traditional Practices*,
https://doi.org/10.1057/978-1-137-53312-8_12

In addition to this, it is also our assessment that affected communities need to do more to challenge these behaviours at a local level. There needs to be an open and honest conversation within communities to acknowledge the existence of these practices and the harm that they cause. In this context appeals by supporters and apologists alike to tradition, religion or culture as justifications, do not hide the significant harm done by these practices and the fundamental abuse of human rights that they represent.

Whilst, as we have highlighted, there has been some pockets of excellent practice there has been compartmentalisation of FGM, forced marriage, witchcraft and faith-based abuse, breast ironing and honour-based abuse. This has meant that some professionals, politicians and others do not see the links across the spectrum of offences and abuses. These offences are rarely committed in isolation; rarely are they single events involving a single perpetrator. Instead and in contrast to other forms of inter-personal violent offences, harmful traditional practices often involve many perpetrators and conspirators.[1]

Professionals must be equipped to identify such offending by providing victims and survivors with the requisite wrap-around support that they need. We maintain that public authorities must also provide longer term support to them especially given the wide range of health consequences and deep psychological impact of harmful traditional practices. Too often services are either non-existent or are short-term fixes that ignore these long-term consequences.

The Future

Moving forward, how best can we respond to the challenge presented by harmful traditional practices? There are a number of areas, which we believe are fundamental to achieving a better understanding of the scale, scope and seriousness of harmful traditional practices, for improving the effectiveness of responses designed to identify victims and survivors for conducting timely interventions and ultimately, to prevent these forms of abuse. We consider each of these below.

---

[1] The UN Secretary General's in-depth study of all forms of violence against women A/61/122/Add.1 (2006), pp. 29–30, paras. 69–77.

1. Terminology

There has been much discourse on the use of terminology particularly the word *honour* in the context of violent abuse, and the terms *practicing communities* and *affected communities* to label communities where harmful traditional practices occur. In this section we consider these issues and provide recommendations as to the best use of terminology.

We have argued throughout this book that honour-based abuse (HBA) is the best overarching description for the range of crimes (violence or otherwise) and abuses perpetrated in the name of honour. The word honour is well entrenched in the academic and other discourse in the area of harmful traditional practices and is widely understood by communities, policy makers and academics. Given this it is important that we are consistent in our collective use of terminology so that victims and survivors fully understand what it is and understand what to do if they have concerns or feel threatened by HBA.

The use of language to describe those communities apparently involved in a particular, or a basket of harmful traditional practices is exceptionally important. There is an abundance of discourse, which refers to the phrase *practising communities*. The authors believe that this phrase stigmatises communities and individuals within those communities as it can be perceived that all individuals from such communities either practice or condone harmful practices. This clearly is not the case. Instead as we have argued in this book, the authors advocate for the use of the phrase *affected communities*. These are communities where there is evidence that *some* members within that community have been victimised or undertake the harmful traditional practice. Indeed, it is important to note that there are many courageous women, men and young people from affected communities who have challenged these practices and been at the forefront of change.

2. Data

There is a need for a reliable source of data concerning the prevalence and characteristics of harmful traditional practices. This is crucial for the design of policy and practice strategies. It would inform on the true scale of offending and allow more accurate estimates of the prevalence of the various types of harmful traditional practice. This would in turn inform the commissioning of adequate specialist services, targeting of service provision to victims and where they are most needed, and ensuring the deployment of multiagency partnership resources to proactively engage affected communities.

The dataset should be at the incident level, with fields in the dataset to record information about the characteristics of an event, perpetrator(s) and victim(s). It should have the capacity to link together different offences, victims/survivors and offenders, this is suggested because these practices are seldom single incidents with single offenders. The dataset should be built from various sources including both government and non-government agencies as each has data the other is not privy to, and each source may have additional information about the same case.

3. Training

Lack of knowledge and experience of working with harmful traditional practices means that training for professionals is imperative. Public authority officials and others working with victims and survivors need to be familiar with the warning signs and trigger events associated with harmful traditional practices and may be associated with an escalation in risk of harm for the victim. In addition, professionals need to understand that victims and survivors are exposed to further risks from the perpetrator(s) and others when they or other witnesses report their experience.[2] The approach taken towards victim(s) is fundamental to reducing victim fear and securing the trust and confidence of victim(s). This allows victims and survivors to feel safe to come forward and report their experiences and to continue to support an investigation and prosecution. It is therefore critical that training must also include how to respond effectively to victims and survivors, manage their needs and manage the risk that they face and effective strategies to protect them from further harm.

4. Sentencing Guidelines

There are no specific sentencing guidelines for crimes associated with harmful traditional practices. As we have argued, developing sentencing guidelines is of some importance given the distinctiveness of offending associated with harmful traditional practices and the risk of inconsistency in sentencing.

---

[2] Hester et al., Victim/survivor voices – a participatory research project, Report for Her Majesty's Inspectorate of Constabulary Honour-based violence inspection (University of Bristol, 2015).

Government should therefore consider setting sentencing guidelines for harmful traditional practices as a priority.

We note however that there has been a shift in the UK Government's approach to the severity of offences committed in a domestic setting resulting in the Sentencing Council publishing guidelines; effective from 24 May 2018, setting out the principles relevant to sentencing cases involving domestic abuse. The guideline, whilst recognising that there is no specific offence of domestic abuse, uses the UK Government's definition of domestic abuse, which includes so-called honour-based abuse, female genital mutilation (FGM) and forced marriage. It details guidance on assessing seriousness, aggravating and mitigating factors and other factors influencing sentencing. The guideline notes that a court should consider, where available, a Victim Personal Statement that will help it to assess the immediate and long-term, physical and psychological effects of the abuse on the victim (and any children, where relevant). Importantly, the guidance also notes that the absence of a VPS should not be taken to indicate the absence of harm.

The above is to be welcomed. However, we also argue that the time is right for a specific guideline, which recognises the distinct nature of harmful traditional practices to ensure consistency of sentencing and approach.

5. Forced Marriage Protection Orders and Female Genital Mutilation Protection Orders

Forced Marriage Protection Orders (FMPOs) and Female Genital Mutilation Protection Orders (FGMPOs) are essential tools in the tactical armoury of professionals to prevent crimes and protect victims and survivors, and there is evidence of the increasing use of these orders. However, one challenge is that these orders can be obtained by a number of sources including the victim, local authorities, civil society organisations and others. As such it is very important to have a consistent process in place to record the orders and the conditions attached, which are readily accessible to all interested parties, especially the police so that they can have adequate oversight of them and to ensure compliance.

At present, some orders obtained by some victims and survivors and civil society organisations are not being notified to the police service. We therefore recommend that Her Majesty's Courts and Tribunal Service (HMCTS) should automatically and securely communicate any such order(s) to the relevant police force(s) on the date that it is granted. The police force should then make arrangements for the orders to be placed onto the UK Police National Computer (PNC) and the UK Police National (Intelligence) Database (PND) to ensure that a centrally accessible record is maintained. This is particularly important in the event that those mentioned in the order move policing area.

6. Experts

In the UK the National Crime Agency (NCA) maintains the list of experts who will provide their expertise to investigating officers, legal and justice professionals. To make best use of this expertise we recommend that the NCA should continue to engage broadly with qualified experts and attempt to influence those with expertise in harmful traditional practices (HTP) to be part of the database. We also recommend that all police forces, CPS, and Public Authorities maintain and share the details of all Gender Based Abuse and HTP experts with their managers and staff

As demonstrated in the stated case of B and G (children) (no2) V Leeds City Council[3] it is vital to ensure that the right expert with the right knowledge is selected depending on the circumstances. This will provide clarity on those areas where there is a paucity of expertise and prompt the identification of UK National and International experts. Such a database will also be complementary to knowledge hubs such as The Global Policing Database[4] and Europol's e-library.[5] Training for said experts could also be made available so that they are familiar with the court and police expectations of experts and their responsibilities.

7. Community-Driven Solutions

Professionals face a real challenge in developing an understanding of the changing communities that they serve. Nevertheless, professionals do need to develop knowledge of the context, drivers and motivation for the commission of harmful traditional practices that can only be gained through engagement with communities and relevant specialist training.

---

[3] B and G (Children) [2014] EWFC 43.
[4] http://whatworks.college.police.uk/About/News/Pages/Database.aspx accessed on 4 November 2017.
[5] https://www.cepol.europa.eu/science-research/e-library accessed on 4 November 2017.

Whilst legislation, public policy, arrests and prosecutions are exceptionally important in preventing and tackling harmful traditional practices, they will not by themselves achieve their sustained eradication. Notions of honour can shape and define attitudes, beliefs and ways of life for individuals, families and communities. These can be so deeply ingrained that individuals and communities must themselves want to eliminate honour and other related harmful traditional practices. The proactive involvement of affected communities, then, alongside the other measures is fundamental to lasting change.

That said, the onus must not solely rest on the shoulders of affected communities but in partnership with government and other professions in developing community-driven solutions.

It is important to note that community-driven solutions are not about mediation or about accessing communities through gatekeepers or alternative dispute resolution mediums, such as Beth Din or Shari'a Courts. Such mechanisms present a number of challenges that can inadvertently undermine the best intentions for community-driven solutions. This is because many of these mechanisms are often led by men and can be institutionally discriminatory towards women, undermining their rights. Successful solutions must therefore involve the whole community incorporating checks and balances such as independent or lay membership and appeals processes built into tribunals.

Harmful traditional practices are steeped within notions of patriarchy and control of women and girls, especially their sexual autonomy. HBA, forced marriage, FGM and other harmful practices disproportionately affect women and girls and are perpetrated mainly by men. As such these practices cannot be sustainably eradicated without engaging and educating men of all ages.[6] It is therefore essential that men and boys from affected communities and the wider community are engaged and have a visible role in taking positive action, standing up and speaking out to prevent and tackle these abuses. Similarly, it is important for women, particularly mothers, to have a role in the education of their male children about the harm these practices do. A powerful recent example of this is the international UK-led Big Brother Movement, which emerged following the first Summit on FGM in December 2016. This movement has developed an increasing international coalition of men to motivate and empower other men and boys to stand up, speak out and take positive proactive action to end gender-based violence towards women and girls.

---

[6] The UN Secretary General's in-depth study of all forms of violence against women, A/61/122/Add.1 (2006), pp. 29–30, paras. 69–77.

8. Specialist Support for Victims and Survivors

The unique nature of harmful traditional practices, and the consequent longer-term health impacts on victims and survivors, is such that specialist support services need to be provided for the medium to longer term support of victims and survivors. It is vital that healthcare providers ensure that there is early intervention in these cases to prevent the health condition of victims and survivors deteriorating. In addition, for some campaigners such effects are also compounded by being a lone voice acting outside the honour parameters set by communities and families with the potential for significant negative health effects, and the threat of additional harm from others.

9. Female Genital Cosmetic Surgery

Female Genital Cosmetic Surgery (FGCS) remains a very real and contentious issue, so clarification of the law is urgently required to assist professionals. One study has found that girls as young as 15 are asking their general practitioners (GPs) about genital cosmetic surgery, and are increasingly concerned that their genitals don't look normal.[7] The Royal College of Obstetricians and Gynaecologists said that cosmetic genital operations should not be carried out on girls under 18, after figures showed that hundreds had such surgery on the UK National Health Service.

Whilst campaigners have sought to prevent affected communities from practising FGM, FGCS is available in private cosmetic clinics to young girls with the consent of their parents and to those over the age of 18. We contend that the parents who support FGCS of their daughters are effectively supporting the practice of FGM on them. FGCS, we assert, falls within the FGM offences outlined in the Female Genital Mutilation Act 2003 as drafted. The current legislation applies both to women and girls and, aside from the recent amendments introduced by the Serious Crime Act 2015, is not age specific and further does not affect the principal primary offence of FGM according to English law.

In 2015, the Home Affairs Select Committee (HASC)[8] called on the UK's government to state specifically that FGCS would be a criminal offence to

---

[7] Simonis M, Manocha R, Ong JJ Female genital cosmetic surgery: a cross-sectional survey exploring knowledge, attitude and practice of general practitioners *BMJ Open* 2016; 6:e 013010. https://doi.org/10.1136/bmjopen-2016-013010.

[8] Home Affairs Select Committee Report, 'Female genital mutilation: follow-up' March 2015.

address the perceived ambiguity over the scope of the law. In the most recent Home Affairs Select Committee (HASC) inquiry examining FGM in parliamentary session 2016/17, the issue of FGCS was not formally addressed. Lack of clarity here is significant as it undermines attempts to end the practice of FGM elsewhere.

Final Comments

Despite the best intentions of the international community, women and girls (and some men and boys) the world over are too often subjected to the worst kinds of abuse. Treated as second-class citizens, their rights are ignored, their opportunities curtailed, their bodies disfigured, their suffering disregarded and their lives sometimes ended. Sadly, as we have seen in this book, much of this abuse is driven by appeals to tradition, culture and religion in the perpetration of harmful traditional practices. It is in equal measure both tragic and frustrating that, in the twenty-first century, we are so far away from eradicating these practices and that there remain many supporters of and apologists for them. Indeed, there remains widespread ignorance about these practices and too many governments and others turn a blind eye to these abuses. It is to be hoped that the brave victims/survivors who campaign daily to raise awareness and affect lasting change will ultimately be heard by everyone and their voices will lead to lasting change.

We hope that this book will make a difference. That it has achieved our aims of informing the reader about harmful traditional practices and identifying ways in which they can be effectively prevented. Indeed, it is our strong hope that this book serves as one small step in the long road to permanently eradicating these terrible abusive practices.

Appendix: World Health Organisation Classification of Female Genital Mutilation[1]

Type I—Partial or total removal of the clitoris and/or the prepuce (clitoridectomy).

When it is important to distinguish between the major variations of Type I mutilation, the following sub-divisions are proposed:

Type Ia, removal of the clitoral hood or prepuce only;
Type Ib, removal of the clitoris with the prepuce.

Type II—Partial or total removal of the clitoris and the labia minora, with or without excision of the labia majora (excision). When it is important to distinguish between the major variations that have been documented, the following sub-divisions are proposed:

Type IIa, removal of the labia minora only;
Type IIb, partial or total removal of the clitoris and the labia minora;
Type IIc, partial or total removal of the clitoris, the labia minora and the labia majora.

Type III—Narrowing of the vaginal orifice with creation of a covering seal by cutting and appositioning the labia minora and/or the labia majora, with or without excision of the clitoris (infibulation). When it is important to distinguish between variations in infibulations, the following sub-divisions are proposed:

Type IIIa, removal and apposition of the labia minora;
Type IIIb, removal and apposition of the labia majora.

Type IV—All other harmful procedures to the female genitalia for non-medical purposes, for example: pricking, piercing, incising, scraping and cauterisation.

---

[1] World Health Organisation, Classification of female genital mutilation accessed on 20 August 2017 via http://www.who.int/reproductivehealth/topics/fgm/overview/en/.

© The Author(s) 2020
G. Campbell et al., *Harmful Traditional Practices*,
https://doi.org/10.1057/978-1-137-53312-8

Index[1]

---

[1] Note: Page numbers followed by 'n' refer to notes.

© The Author(s) 2020
G. Campbell et al., *Harmful Traditional Practices*,
https://doi.org/10.1057/978-1-137-53312-8

Lightning Source UK Ltd.
Milton Keynes UK
UKHW022012220322
400453UK00006B/1200